# Unconditional Surrender

## ULYSSES S. GRANT IN THE CIVIL WAR

by Curt Fields
and Chris Mackowski

EMERGING CIVIL WAR SERIES

*Chris Mackowski, series editor*
*Cecily Nelson Zander, chief historian*

# The Emerging Civil War Series

**offers compelling, easy-to-read overviews of some of the Civil War's most important battles and stories.**

*Recipient of the Army Historical Foundation's Lieutenant General Richard G. Trefry Award for contributions to the literature on the history of the U.S. Army*

## Also part of the Emerging Civil War Series:

*Attack at Daylight and Whip Them: The Battle of Shiloh, April 6–7, 1862* by Gregory A. Mertz

*Dreams of Victory: General P. G. T. Beauregard in the Civil War* by Sean Michael Chick

*Glorious Courage: John Pelham in the Civil War* by Sarah Kay Bierle

*A Grand Opening Squandered: The Battle for Petersburg, June 15–18, 1864* by Sean Michael Chick

*Grant's Last Battle: The Story Behind the Personal Memoirs of Ulysses S. Grant* by Chris Mackowski

*Hell Itself: The Battle of the Wilderness, May 5–7, 1864* by Chris Mackowski

*Hurricane from the Heavens: The Battle of Cold Harbor, May 26–June 5, 1864* by Daniel T. Davis and Phillip S. Greenwalt

*John Brown's Raid: Harpers Ferry and the Coming of the Civil War, October 16–18, 1859* by Jon-Erik M. Gilot and Kevin R. Pawlak

*Man of Fire: William Tecumseh Sherman in the Civil War* by Derek D. Maxfield

*The Most Desperate Acts of Gallantry: George A. Custer in the Civil War* by Daniel T. Davis

*Passing Through the Fire: Joshua Lawrence Chamberlain in the Civil War* by Brian F. Swartz

*A Season of Slaughter: The Battle of Spotsylvania Court House, May 8–21, 1864* by Chris Mackowski and Kristopher D. White

*Strike Them a Blow: Battle along the North Anna River, May 21–25, 1864* by Chris Mackowski

*To the Bitter End: Appomattox, Bennett Place, and the Surrenders of the Confederacy* by Robert M. Dunkerly

## Other Grant-Related Books by Chris Mackowski:

*The Battle of Jackson, Mississippi, May 14, 1863*

*A Tempest of Iron and Lead: Spotsylvania Court House, May 8–21, 1864*

*The Vicksburg Campaign 1863: Grant's Failed Offensives* (Vol. 1)

*The Vicksburg Campaign 1863: The Inland Battles, Siege and Surrender* (Vol. 2)

*Grant at 200: Reconsidering the Life and Legacy of Ulysses S. Grant* (co-edited with Frank Scaturro, including a contribution by Dr. Curt Fields)

**For a complete list of titles in the Emerging Civil War Series, visit www.emergingcivilwar.com.**

# Unconditional Surrender

## ULYSSES S. GRANT IN THE CIVIL WAR

by Curt Fields
and Chris Mackowski

EMERGING CIVIL WAR SERIES

SB
Savas Beatie
California

First edition, first printing

Library of Congress Cataloging-in-Publication Data

Names: Fields, Curt, 1948- author
Title: Unconditional surrender : Ulysses S. Grant in the Civil War / Curt Fields.
Description: El Dorado Hills, CA : Savas Beatie LLC, 2025. | Series:
    Emerging civil war series | Summary: "Ulysses S. Grant didn't think he'd
    even have an opportunity to get into the war, yet, by the time it ended,
    he commanded every soldier serving in the United States Army. This book
    allows readers to walk in Grant's footsteps with Dr. Curt Fields, the
    nation's foremost Ulysses S. Grant living historian. Distilled within
    these pages are years of extensive study that offer an ideal
    introduction to the "dust-covered man" from the West who won the Civil
    War and saved the United States"-- Provided by publisher.
Identifiers: LCCN 2025020731 | ISBN 9781611217445 paperback | ISBN
    9781611217452 ebook
Subjects: LCSH: Grant, Ulysses S. (Ulysses Simpson), 1822-1885--Military
    leadership | United States--History--Civil War, 1861-1865--Campaigns |
    Generals--United States--Biography | LCGFT: Biographies
Classification: LCC E672 .F54 2025 | DDC 973.8/2092 $a B--dc23/eng/20250618
LC record available at https://lccn.loc.gov/2025020731

SB

Savas Beatie LLC
989 Governor Drive, Suite 101
El Dorado Hills, California 95762
916-941-6896 / sales@savasbeatie.com / www.savasbeatie.com

All Savas Beatie titles are available for bulk purchase discounts. Contact us for details.
Proudly published, printed, and warehoused in the United States of America.

# Dedications

## From Curt:

This book is dedicated to anyone who reads it!
May you put it down with more than when you picked it up.

*and*

To all reenactors and living historians
because they show us how life and war
really looked and sounded to the people
who lived through both.
Thank you all for allowing me
to be a part of what you do.

## From Chris:

To Aaron Chimbel, dean
Jandoli School of Communication
Good friend. Good leader. Good guy.

# Table of Contents

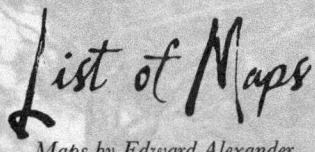

# List of Maps

*Maps by Edward Alexander*

*Footnotes for this volume are available at*
*https://emergingcivilwar.com/publication/footnotes/*

PHOTO CREDITS: Author's Collection/Curt Fields (ac/cf); Author's Collection/Chris Mackowski (ac/cm); *Battles & Leaders of the Civil War* (b&l); *Campaigning with Grant* by Horace Porter (cwg); *The [Louisville, KY] Courier-Journal* (cj); *Harper's Weekly* (hw); Illinois State Archives (isa); Library of Congress (loc); Library of Congress/Carol Highsmith (loc/ch); Shelly Liebler (sl); National Park Service (nps); Mary Beth Perring (mbp); *The Personal Memoirs of Ulysses S. Grant* (us); Buddy Secor (bs); Jake Shane (js); Virginia Museum of History and Culture (vmhc); White House Historical Association (whha)

## For the Emerging Civil War Series

Theodore P. Savas, *publisher*
Sarah Keeney, *editorial consultant*
Veronica Kane, *production supervisor*
MaryBeth Allison, *copyeditor*
Pat McCormick, *proofreader*

Chris Mackowski, *series editor and co-founder*
Cecily Nelson Zander, *chief historian*
Kristopher D. White, *emeritus editor*

Layout by Chris Mackowski

# Acknowledgments

Our combined thanks to our history friend and fellow Grant enthusiast, NPS Ranger Nick Sacco at the Ulysses S. Grant National Historic Site in St. Louis. Nick graciously agreed to write a foreword for the book.

Thanks to Theodore P. Savas for publishing this book and to his staff at Savas Beatie for their work distributing and promoting it. Veronica Kane, as Savas Beatie's production manager for ECW, gets a special shout-out.

Cartographer Edward Alexander made us a set of his always-great maps. Buddy Secor and Shelly Liebler each stepped up to fulfill special photography needs. ECW's Josh Frye helped run down a few last-minute items for us.

**FROM CURT:** I would like to thank Chris Mackowski for his steady encouragement to me and for his contributions to this book. I don't remember how I met Chris—seems like he's always been a friend—but I DO remember that one of the first things he ever said to me was, "Hey, pal! You need to write a book about Grant! Who better to do that than you?"

A special group of people who have materially contributed to my career as a Grant Living Historian is the leadership of (what is now officially) "The Land of U. S. Grant" in his hometown of Georgetown, Ohio. "The Land of U. S. Grant," under the auspices of The Ohio Historical Connection, encompasses Grant's Boyhood home, his father's tannery building and the Dutch Hill school he attended for the first six years of his education. They selected me as their official Grant in 2015, and I have had the pleasure of working with them since then— including, significantly, the Grant bicentennial year. Ned and Sue Lodwick, Stan and Nancy Purdy, and Bud and Joye White have been stalwarts in nurturing the legacy

**"The Leader and His Battles"**
(loc)

of Grant and how his story is told in his hometown. They are people of character and have been supportive and informative good friends of Grant and me.

Lena Moody is due many thanks for her support, from the beginning, of my portrayal of General and President Grant. Thousands of miles have slid past the windshield as she has trundled up and down the highways with me, going to my presentations. She has even, without complaint, listened to most of them.

I also want to look back over my shoulder and warmly thank Ms. Betty Hendon. Ms. Hendon was my tenth-grade English teacher at Memphis Technical High School. She firmly told me, "Curtis, you should be a writer!" Then she added the admonition: "But write about what you know about!" Here's to you, Ms. Hendon. Thanks for the confidence you had in a kid in one of your classes and for making the effort to tell him so. You made a life-long impression on that boy.

**Considered a low point in his life, Grant tried selling firewood when he lived in St. Louis.** (nps)

**FROM CHRIS:** My thanks to my friend Curt Fields for taking on this project in the midst of his many other responsibilities. He spends a tremendous amount of time on the road, apostolic in his zeal to preach the Gospel of Grant, so I'm lucky he took this project on and squeezed it in to his busy schedule. Tens of thousands of people a year are lucky that he *has* such a busy schedule because they get to benefit from Curt's insightful portrayal of such a fascinating and important figure.

My own general in chief is Aaron Chimbel, dean of the Jandoli School of Communication at St. Bonaventure University. He gives me great latitude to prosecute my responsibilities, which in turn has allowed me to thrive in a way that, I hope, brings credit back to the Jandoli School. I offer my dedication of this book to him.

Finally, thanks to my wife, Jennifer; my sons, Jackson and Maxwell; and my daughter, Steph, her husband, Thomas, and my granddaughters, Gracie and the Pip. Grant adored his family, and I adore mine.

**PHOTO ON PREVIOUS SPREAD: "It takes a village"—or, in Grant's case, a large staff. Here they are, pictured with the general, at City Point, Virginia, in the summer of 1864.** (loc)

# *Foreword*

## BY NICK SACCO

Perhaps no other military or political figure during the Civil War knew Ulysses S. Grant on a personal level as well as William T. Sherman. In a letter from 1879, Sherman recalled that he had known Grant well before the war "as a cadet at West Point, as a lieutenant of the Fourth Infantry, as a citizen of St. Louis, and as a growing general all through a bloody civil war." As civilians, both men grew up in Ohio, raised their families in St. Louis, endured personal tragedy, and experienced financial struggles. As military generals, both men experienced their fair share of initial skepticism from the Lincoln administration and controversy in the press. They nevertheless persevered to achieve battlefield victory as the Union's ultimate fighting duo. And yet, Sherman looked back at more than 30 years of friendship and admitted that Grant "is a strange character . . . to me he is a mystery, and I believe he is a mystery to himself." If Sherman was right about Grant's inability to figure himself out, how can we expect scholars, educators, and students today to get any closer to understanding who the real Ulysses S. Grant was?

This conundrum has not stopped people from trying to understand Grant since his death in 1885. Enter living history into the equation. Broadly speaking, living history is the practice of portraying historic people or composite characters through period clothing and dramatic performance. Some performers practice living history in third person; they speak in the present tense about the past and play the role of an educator in historic clothing. Others take on the daunting task of doing first person interpretations, creating elaborate performances that channel the look, feel, tone, sound, and mannerisms of the historic figures we read about in books. Whether it's Grant, Sherman, Robert E. Lee, Clara Barton, Harriet Tubman Davis, or any other figure from the Civil War era, there has been no lack of interest in creating an imaginative past for audiences through living history.

**Curt Fields as Ulysses S. Grant and Thomas Jessee as Robert E. Lee exiting the McLean house at the Appomattox 150th commemoration.** (ac/cf)

During the Civil War Centennial in the 1960s, living history played a central role in educational programming throughout the country. Sometimes it took the form of battle reenactments, where thousands of living history soldiers donned their replica Civil War uniforms to recreate scenes at Gettysburg, Vicksburg, Chancellorsville, and elsewhere. These reenactments captivated audiences and left an enduring legacy for the future of Civil War education in public history settings. For example, Millard Crane, a New York resident who attended a reenactment of the First Battle of Bull Run with his family on July 22 and 23, 1961, later recalled that "we had never witnessed anything like it . . . It had been so well rehearsed . . . all seemed to catch one up into *a sense of living history* and one could almost feel it was 1861."

At other times living history takes on the form of an individual or group performance covering a wide range of topics, including life in the camp, life in the home front, or political debates. While battle reenactments are prohibited at most battlefields today with rare exceptions, living history performances have continued to play a vital role at local, state, and nationally designated historic sites that interpret the Civil War. Go to the website of any prominent Civil War site today and you'll most likely find a living history performance on the upcoming events calendar.

Many people have portrayed Ulysses S. Grant over the years. One of the finest performers among them is Dr. Curt Fields. Watching Dr. Fields in a first-person performance is a sort of time-traveling adventure. Like Millard Crane, I find myself enamored with a sense of living history that transports me back to the Civil War era when watching him. Dr. Fields certainly looks the part and—while we'll never know for certain—he sounds the part too. But most importantly, Dr. Fields *knows* the part. As a veteran educator and researcher long before his living history days, Dr. Fields has undertaken an admirable effort to master his craft since beginning to portray Grant in 2010. He has as good an understanding of the Grant historiography as any Civil War scholar yet remains a dedicated student anxious to learn more.

I also admire how Dr. Fields portrays Grant as a multi-dimensional person who experienced difficult struggle and stunning success alike. While this book is primarily focused on Grant's generalship, Dr. Fields is comfortable portraying Grant to current students at West Point as a representative of the Class of 1843, as a struggling St. Louis farmer to audiences at Ulysses S. Grant National Historic Site, and as an author facing insurmountable health issues during a visit to Ulysses S. Grant Cottage National Historic Landmark in New York. His humane approach to Grant's life helps audiences around the county learn more about a farmer, general, and president who was seemingly a mystery to himself.

To tell these important stories, Dr. Fields has teamed up with Chris Mackowski, a prolific writer and scholar in his own right, to offer an exploration of Ulysses S. Grant's generalship. Dr. Mackowski's wide range of Civil War scholarship, including thoughtful examinations of Grant's Overland Campaign and his last days while writing his *Personal Memoirs*, makes him a respected scholar among Grant historians, me included. Together, they have produced an introductory study that allows readers of all ages to find something useful about Ulysses S. Grant. Those of us who are students of the Civil War will benefit from walking in Grant's footsteps with Dr. Curt Fields and Dr. Chris Mackowski as our guides.

**Curt helped West Point kick off its "Year of Grant" commemoration for the U. S. Grant bicentennial.** (ac/cf)

NICK SACCO, *a historian based in St. Louis, has written extensively about Ulysses S. Grant and the Civil War era. He works at Ulysses S. Grant National Historic Site. The views expressed in the foreword are his and do not represent the views of the Department of the Interior or the National Park Service.*

# Introduction

## BY CURT FIELDS

My friend (and co-author/editor) Chris Mackowski shocked me with his exclamation, "Hey, Pal! You should write a book!" I was taken aback and more than a bit overwhelmed. I could only think to say, "Me?"

Chris laughed and asked, "Who better than you?"

With that encouragement, I was off on an odyssey that put to paper the studies that have prepared me for portraying Grant—and, in a measure, my experiences *as* Grant to write this narrative *about* Grant in the Civil War. It is a look, from the inside out, at what he did and why.

I have studied Grant closely for more than a decade, reading primary and secondary sources—many of them multiple times. I have walked most of the places and battlefields where Grant walked. By doing so, have felt a deep closeness with him. I wasn't walking the ground with an intent to write a book but rather to get a sense of what he saw that might then help me add greater breadth to my presentations. My feelings on those walks have always been strong. Trying to match his descriptions and "see" battlefields or places as he did is akin to focusing a stereoscope card, bringing two images together to see one image with depth and detail.

Writing a sweeping narrative about Grant and his battles in the war was tempting. However, "sweeping" and "dynamic" were not in his vocabulary. I wanted a more personal perspective.

Grant was a mystery to people who knew him, and he has been a mystery to the subsequent generations that have read about him. Sherman said he thought Grant was a mystery even to himself and predicted 10,000 years or so would pass before Grant would be understood and maybe not even then.

As I learned about him, for instance, it was a surprise to discover that Grant had a great sense of humor and that he was a devoted and indulgent father. I was equally surprised to learn that he would much rather capture a man than wound or kill him. His determination to win in battle was steely, yet his humanity to the killed, wounded, and captured was profound.

Grant was reluctant to write about himself and, for years, resisted suggestions to write his memoirs. Circumstances eventually forced his hand, but for the longest time, he was leery of the idea. It brings

to mind a quote I like from President Lincoln, which is a sentiment I think Grant shared: "Biographies, as generally written, are not only misleading but false. The author makes a wonderful hero of his subject. He magnifies his perfections, if he has any, and suppresses his imperfections. History is not history unless it is the truth."

I am certainly a Grant enthusiast, but I am not a Grant apologist. He had his flaws and foibles, of which I am painfully aware. But it's because he was wonderfully human and complex.

What I have written here about what Grant will, I hope, give the reader some insight into what he did and why.

Curt speaks to thousands of people across the country each year. Here, he addresses an audience in southern Ohio's "Land of Grant," the area where a young Hiram Ulysses Grant grew up. (ac/cf)

Grant told his brother Orvil as they were walking home from an evening recruiting rally in Galena, Illinois, days after the war started, "I am in to do all I can."

I have been as well.

*   *   *

*What follows are the most-frequently asked questions
Curt gets during his presentations about Grant.*

### How would you address questions about Grant's drinking?

Grant was a man who had a problem *with* alcohol, not *for* alcohol, and the Grand Canyon lies between those two prepositions. A problem with alcohol describes Grant's condition. He said himself that more than one drink will make his speech slurred—so we're talking two drinks—and more than two drinks will make him unsteady on his feet.

And it hit him like a locomotive, really hard and really fast. Physiologically, he could not process alcohol.

**FROM CHRIS:** Let me put my editorial hat on for a moment rather than my authorial hat. "Being" Grant has given Curt an insightful way of knowing and understanding a man who has a historical reputation as a sphinx. I wanted to capture Curt's unique position, at least in part, by using photos of Curt as Grant throughout the book as illustrations. I also thought this would be a way to help put Curt's personal stamp on this biography. I make this point because less charitable critics might think it presumptuous of Curt to use his own photos in the book; the idea—and any such blame that might be attached to it—is my own. If there is credit to be had from the idea, I direct it all to Curt and the many talented photographers who have worked with him over the years to help channel and capture Grant's essence.

Dialogue in the text that appears in quotation marks has been quoted directly from a source. On occasion, where a source indirectly quotes a person's speech, we have put that dialogue in *italics* rather than in quotation marks. That has allowed us to convey the sense of what a person said without misrepresenting their words as exact quotations.

Did he drink occasionally? He did. But he did not have a problem *for* alcohol. That would indicate addiction: "I've got to have it." Grant was never like that. But of course, that reputation that haunts him.

### Why do you think Grant was successful?

He was self driven. He was self confident. He never gave up hope. He always felt there would be another day. But you couldn't just wait around for it, wait for something to happen. That was not Grant. He always felt you had to be busy. He always was driven to work and be productive

Hidden under his self-effacing, quiet demeanor, he was a brilliant military strategist and tactician—and it's hard to be both, but he was both. Once he got the opportunity to show what he could do, there was no stopping him.

### What did Grant want to do that he couldn't?

Take Mobile. He advocated three different times—after Donelson, after Shiloh and the taking of Corinth, and after Vicksburg—to go to Mobile, Alabama. And he was never allowed to. And so Mobile never fell until the final weeks of the war, in mid-April 1865 after Appomattox. But the way Grant saw it, if Mobile had fallen sooner, it quite possibly could have shortened the war.

### What did Grant like to eat?

His favorite breakfast was sliced cucumber dipped in cold pickle brine. I think that's because his tongue and mouth were so coated with nicotine that it took something that pungent and that sharp to cut through the coated taste buds so that he could taste anything!

"The art of war
is simple enough. . . .

Find out where your enemy is.
Get at him as soon as you can.
Strike him as hard as you can,
and keep moving on."

— *Ulysses S. Grant*

# *Prologue*

The last time Ulysses S. Grant had seen Simon Bolivar Buckner had been at the Dover Hotel on the banks of the Cumberland River. Grant had just accepted Buckner's unconditional surrender of the garrison inside Fort Donelson.

That had been February 16, 1862, some 23 years earlier. Now it was July 10, 1885, and here was Bucker, with his luxuriant mustache now snow white, climbing the steps of the wooden porch where Grant sat under the eaves in a wicker chair. Barely able to speak because of agonizing throat cancer, Grant had taken to scribbling what he had to say on slips of paper. "I appreciate your calling very highly," Grant penciled. "You look very natural, except that your hair has whitened, and you have grown stouter."

It was the kind of good-natured ribbing only old friends can appreciate. Indeed, the two men had known each other since their days together at West Point. Grant graduated in 1843, a year ahead of Buckner. The two comrades served together in the Mexican War, and together they had climbed the volcano Popocatepetl, one of Mexico's tallest peaks.

In 1854, Grant left the army under a cloud. Stationed on the West Coast, he traveled south to

*The Overlook at Mt. McGregor still offers a beautiful spot for sunrises and contemplation.* (ac/cf)

A native of Kentucky, Simon Bolivar Buckner graduated in the West Point Class of 1844, a year behind Grant. The two served in the same division during the Mexican War and, after hostilities ceased, they hiked the Popocatépetl volcano together. "[W]e were quite well acquainted," Grant wrote of him in his memoirs. (loc)

Nicaragua, crossed the isthmus, and took a steamer to New York, where he ran out of money. Buckner, stationed in New York as a commissary officer, covered for Grant long enough for Grant's family to send the funds that would get him the rest of the way back to Ohio. Grant never forgot the gesture; in fact, following the Confederate surrender at Fort Donelson, Grant pulled Buckner aside and asked if he had enough money to cover his expenses. "Grant tendered me the use of his purse," Buckner recounted. "I did not accept it, of course, but it showed his generosity and his appreciation of my aid to him years before, which was really very little."

After Buckner was exchanged, he served his side honorably for the duration of the war. In May 1865 in New Orleans, he was one of the final Confederate generals to surrender. Following the war, he embarked on a career as a newspaperman in Louisiana and, later, in his home state of Kentucky. Lately, he had set his eye on Bluegrass politics.

Buckner, 62, was in New York state on a honeymoon with his 28-year-old second wife, Delia Claiborne. The couple had first visited Niagara Falls and were lately visiting Saratoga Springs. There, they had met members of Grant's family, who had invited the Buckners to visit the family patriarch at nearby Mt. McGregor on the grounds of the new Balmoral Hotel. Grant's condition had "seemed so easy" that morning, they said, and he would surely welcome the chance to see his old friend.

"I am very glad to see you indeed," Grant scribbled upon their arrival, "and allow me to congratulate you [on your marriage]."

Grant had come to Mt. McGregor for the fresh mountain air under doctors' orders. His throat cancer—the likely result of heavy pipe and cigar smoking his whole adult life—was terminal, and Grant was now in its final stages.

The main thing keeping him alive was a massive writing project—although his wife Julia swore it was killing him. For the past year, Grant had been writing his memoirs, a two-volume project that would be published by none other than Mark Twain's own publishing house. Now, caught as he was between the

PUCK.

For these, who fought, the War is done;
For them life's evening sky
Grows tender o'er a setting sun
Where fires of anger die.
Toward the mountains of the west
They look with peaceful sight;
The storm they braved has sunk to rest,
Into forgetful night.

From foe to friend—from foe to friend!
O consecrated years,
How have ye worked toward this end
Through myriad doubts and fears!
The hand that laid the sword aside
Now seeks the conqueror's hand—
Friends! They are sharers in one pride,
And lovers of one land.

O meaner folk, of narrower souls,
Heirs of ignoble thought,
Stir not the camp-fire's blackened coals
Blood-drenched by those who fought;
Lest out of heaven a fire shall yet
Bear God's own vengeance forth
On those who once again would set
Discord 'twixt South and North.

FORT DONELSON, 1862.    GRANT AND BUCKNER.    MOUNT McGREGOR, 1885.
A Relinke to the "Bloody Shirt" Patriots.

Buckner initially tried to keep his visit to Mt. McGregor a secret. "I declined to be interviewed . . ." he recounted, "and said it was a personal affair between Grant and myself. Soon after this a telegram came . . . saying General Grant desires publicity given to your visit. I understood by that that Grant would be pleased to have the world know I called upon him. . . ." The two old soldiers, proponents of reconciliation, wanted their meeting to serve as an example. (loc)

agony in his throat, the addictive nature of the cocaine used as a pain killer, and sheer exhaustion, Grant toiled under a deadline he knew he could not avoid. "I would have more hope of satisfying the expectation of the public if I could have allowed myself more time," he wrote in his foreword.

Grant had never thought of himself as a writer, and for years he had resisted requests to write his memoirs. He had only taken up the effort after a business partner had swindled him and his entire family of nearly everything. Grant took up the pen as a way to earn money.

But as he wrote, Grant discovered he had something to say.

"My family is American, and has been for generations, in all its branches, direct and collateral," he declared. As the man who rose from obscurity to lead the United States to victory in a civil war defined by sectionalism, such a statement of national identity

**Grant usually wrote in the mornings and spent the afternoon on edits. This now-iconic image was taken in June 1885.** (loc)

on a personal level was a shot across the bow at anyone still worried about North or South.

"I have witnessed since my sickness just what I have wished to see ever since the war: harmony and good feeling between the sections," Grant scribbled in a note to Buckner as they sat on the porch. "I have always contended that if there had been no body left but the soldiers we would have had peace in a year. [Jubal] Early and [D. H.] Hill are the only two that I know of who do not seem to be satisfied on the southern side."

Early and Hill, two malcontented former Confederate generals, may have appeared to Grant to be in the minority, but after his death, they would play an outsized role in tearing down his legacy. As chief architects of what became known as the myth of the Lost Cause, they explained away Southern defeat, in part, by besmirching Grant's reputation at every turn, for decades. And so came accusations of "Grant the Drunk" and "Grant the Butcher" and "Grant the Corrupt, Incompetent President."

Grant would never have anticipated it. He had campaigned for president under the motto, "Let us have peace," and he had no reason to doubt that

Irritable and irrascible— postwar malcontents Daniel Harvey Hill (left) and Jubal Early (right). Former Confederate generals, they served among the principal architects of the Lost Cause interpretation of the war, which bolstered the reputation of Confederate Gen. Robert E. Lee by tearing down the reputation of the man who beat him. (ac/cm) (loc)

outcome now. As he told Buckner, "We may now well look forward to a perpetual peace at home."

Indeed, it had been in that very spirit that Buckner had made his visit. "I wanted him to know the Confederate soldiers appreciated his conduct at every surrender during the war, and after the war in Reconstruction days," Buckner later reported.

After Grant and the Buckners concluded their warm reunion on that July afternoon in 1885, Grant urged his friend to share the news about their meeting. He was dying, it was true—"there cannot be a cure in my case," Grant wrote—but he expected a bright future. Let their friendship serve as an example.

No one on the porch that afternoon knew it, but Grant had less than two weeks to live.

# Grant Takes Command

## CHAPTER ONE
### *April–July 1861*

Ulysses S. Grant was afraid he would miss the war.

He was days away from his thirty-ninth birthday when the war broke out, toiling unhappily in his father's leather-goods shop in Galena, Illinois. It was the latest in a line of unspectacular careers Grant had undertaken during his seven years as a civilian.

Prior to that, though, he had served as an officer in the United States Army—and had been a war hero at that. He had graduated 21st out of 39 cadets in the West Point Class of 1843 and, like so many of his classmates, served in the war against Mexico. During the final assault on Mexico City, Grant manhandled an artillery piece to the top of a church steeple and blasted one of the gates to the city. The act of valor earned him a brevet promotion to captain.

Postwar assignments along the Great Lakes, in Panama, and on the West Coast took him far from home and his young wife, Julia, whom he had married in August 1848 when he returned to St. Louis from the Mexican War. In 1852, when he transferred with the U.S. 4th Infantry to the Pacific Northwest, he couldn't afford to bring his wife and two children on the pay of a lieutenant. He went without them, but troubles with loneliness then led to troubles with

**Grant's time at White Haven in St. Louis were his "lean years," yet they did much to forge his character.** (ac/cf)

**ILLINOIS, 1861—** Grant had lived in Illinois less than a year before civil war broke out, but he had spent considerable time in St. Louis during his early service in the U.S. Army. By the end of 1861, he had traversed much of the state as he settled into his wartime responsibilities.

Jesse Grant worked in the leather industry for most of his life. When his young family lived in Georgetown, Ohio, he owned a tannery. In Galena, Illinois, he owned a leathergoods store, Grant & Perkins (left), although Jesse mostly left daily operations to his sons. (ac/cm)

alcohol. Under a cloud, Grant resigned from the army on April 11, 1854, after he had been promoted to full captain.

Back in St. Louis, Grant tried farming. To make ends meet while clearing the trees from his farm, he sold the timber, peddling it as firewood for $4 per cord. After five unproductive years, he gave up on farming and joined a partnership to sell real estate and collect rents. That, too, was unsuccessful.

During the grim winter of 1859, Captain Grant (as he was generally known) gave up on that partnership and asked his father, Jesse, for help. Jesse offered him a job working for his two younger brothers in Galena, Illinois. In April of 1860, he, Julia, and their (now) four young children boarded a steamboat at the St. Louis wharf and headed upriver. At age 38, Grant was starting over, working in the family leather business he hated, but he had a job and poverty had been averted.

The Grants rented a two-story brick house for $100 a year. It sat high atop a bluff north of Main Street; to reach it required a climb up several

A historic plaque marks the former location of Grant & Perkins in downtown Galena. (mbp)

On their arrival in Illinois, Ulysses and Julia Grant rented a bluff-top house north of Main Street. Julia described Galena as "a charming, bustling town settled in the rich ore-laden hills of northern Illinois. The atmosphere was so cool and dry, the sun shone so brightly, that it gave us the impression of a smiling welcome.... She has greeted us with open arms. I have only pleasant, kindly memories of this home." (loc)

Attorney John Rawlins would play a pivotal role in Grant's professional life. In the wake of Fort Sumter, Grant and Rawlins raised troops together. "This is no longer a question of politics," Rawlins said at one event. "It is simply country or no country." Following Grant's elevation to brigadier general, he appointed Rawlins his chief of staff—a position he would hold for the war's duration. (loc)

hundred wooden steps. The family "lived so quietly, so inconspicuously," settling into a "quiet routine," according to an early biographer. Grant was thankful to have a way to support his wife and kids, but he loathed the work.

Just a year later, civil war erupted. On April 12, South Carolinians fired on Fort Sumter, a Federal installation at the mouth of Charleston Harbor. On April 15, President Abraham Lincoln called for 75,000 volunteers to suppress the rebellion. On April 16, following a public meeting in Galena, Grant resolved to join the war effort. "I thought I was done with soldiering," he admitted to his youngest brother, Orvil, as they walked home from the meeting. "I never expected to be in the military again. But I was educated by the Government; and if my knowledge and experience can be of service, I think I ought to offer them." Orvil agreed.

One of the speakers that night had been a local attorney, John Rawlins. "I have been a Democrat all my life; but this is no longer a question of politics. It is simply Union or disunion, country or no country . . ." Rawlins thundered. "We will stand by the flag of our country and appeal to the God of Battles!" This closely reflected Grant's view. For him, the Union cause transcended politics. "There are but two parties now," he privately told his father, "Traitors and Patriots." He would go to war to save the country—although he did admit in a letter to his pro-slavery father-in-law, Col. Frederick Dent, "In all this I can see but the doom of slavery." The colonel's views had impacted Grant deeply during their time living together at the Dent home of White Haven in St. Louis, but Galena was quite different: "a hotbed of Republican discussion and agitation," according to Grant biographer Ronald C. White.

Congressman Elihu Washburne, a Republican who represented the area around Galena, was a close ally of Lincoln's. He knew of Grant's distinguished Mexican War experience. He also suspected Grant's Democratic leanings, although Grant had been unable to actually vote in the previous year's election because he hadn't yet met the state's residency requirement. In Washburne's eyes, this gave Grant what biographer Ron Chernow described as a "bipartisan veneer." Washburne believed having someone from a different part of the political spectrum would lend credibility to the recruitment effort.

On April 18, men from around Galena gathered for another rally where Washburne gave a rousing, patriotic oration. Then—in a surprise move—he nominated Grant to serve as the chair of the recruiting meeting. Grant, sitting in the back of the room "in grave silence," was shocked to hear his name called. He rose with much embarrassment and made his way to the front of the room. He had the look of "a serious, capable, sympathetic country doctor" with "a certain impressiveness," recounted one writer. "[H]is face thoughtful and resolute. He wore a full beard, light brown in color, trimmed rather close, and the firm line of his lips could be seen."

Rather than giving the crowd a rousing stemwinder of a speech as Washburne had done, Grant spoke calmly, level-headedly, honestly. "The army is not a picnicking party. Nor is it an excursion," he warned the crowd. "You will have hard fare." His sober assessment deflated the meeting's "bombast," replacing it with "genuine, resolute patriotism." Twenty-two men enlisted on the spot. Another eighteen joined the following day. Grant, John Rawlins, and several friends barnstormed the county to raise more recruits, and within a week, he had a full company, the Jo Daviess Guards, named after the county. Grant issued the men pine sticks to use as guns, and he drilled the Guard in Washburne's wide front yard.

"Mr. [Elihu] Washburne, allow me to thank you for the part you have taken in giving me my present position," Grant wrote to the Congressman who became his invaluable political patron. "I think I see your hand in it and admit that I had no personal claims for your kind office in the matter. I can assure you however my whole heart is in the cause which we are fighting for and I pledge myself that if equal to the task before me you shall never have cause to regret the part you have taken." (loc)

The March 27, 1869, issue of *Frank Leslie's Illustrated Newspaper* conjured the scene of Grant's 1861 departure for war. "It was his first step to fame and to the Presidential chair," the paper proclaimed. "As, clad in well-worn citizen's dress, with carpet-bag in hand, he was leaving his residence on the hill, with no higher hope, perhaps, than the command of a company, a woman residing in the neighborhood passed that way and asked him where he was going. 'I am going to Springfield to offer my services to President Lincoln,' was the answer. He never returned to Galena until after his appointment as Lieutenant-General." (fl)

When the company tried to elect Grant their captain, he declined. "I have been graduated at West Point," he told them, "I have been a Captain in the regular army and I should have a Colonelcy or a proper staff appointment—nothing else would be proper." It wasn't a boast; Grant understood his worth in a time of military emergency. He hoped the governor would furnish something appropriate. In the meantime, he made himself as useful as possible, teaching the recruits the basics of military discipline and teaching the officers how to be officers.

On April 25, the Galena recruits—sporting fresh new uniforms made from cloth Grant had picked out himself—prepared to ship out to the state capital in Springfield to muster into Federal service as an eventual part of the 11th Illinois. Citizens flocked to the streetside to watch the march toward the train station, escorted by the local fire company, the Masonic society, the order of Odd Fellows, and a gaggle of local officials. Grant, "with a lean carpet-bag in his hand, stood modestly in the crowd on the sidewalk" and watched them pass, falling in at the end.

Springfield "seethed like a pot with orators and soldiers and place-seekers and glory-hunters," said one writer. Grant hoped for an appointment to some command or other by the governor, yet he did not look at all the part of a military man. One witness described Grant as "seedy": "he had only one suit and that he had worn all winter—his short pipe, his grizzled beard and old slouch hat did not make him look like a promising candidate for a colonel." Governor Yates's secretery rebuffed him. "Call again," he said.

Lacking connections beyond Washburne—who was not on especially friendly terms with Yates—and unwilling to shamelessly promote himself, Grant found his new-found military career over almost as soon as it had started. "I was perfectly sickened at the political wire-pulling for all these commissions and would not engage in it," he wrote his father. As he prepared to return to Galena, though, a last-minute call from the governor led to a staff appointment that took good advantage of Grant's military experience.

There were few such military men around, and Grant's former service as a quartermaster and commissary officer made him instantly invaluable because no one in the adjutant general's office even knew how to requisition supplies. Grant taught procedures and protocols from the ground up. He hated the busy work, but everyone recognized his competence and insight, which almost doomed him as too valuable to promote. "[A]nyone could ask any military question whatsoever of him and receive a clear, concise, and unforgettable answer," claimed one writer.

But a fluke incident a few weeks later opened another door: a fellow officer, discontented about an expected promotion that didn't come through, resigned in a huff, and Grant found himself in temporary command of one of the military encampments around the capital. That, in turn, led to a renewed look from Yates, who soon put Grant in command of the state's mustering-in efforts: as new recruits assembled, Grant oversaw their onboarding and initial training. He was so successful at the work that the regiment in Mattoon renamed its camp "Camp Grant" in his honor.

Yet no coveted colonelcy came. Too antsy to get involved, too worried that he'd miss out, Grant then broke his own rule: He began to seek out advancement. He tried another direct appeal to Yates. No luck. He made an appeal in Missouri. No luck. He appealed to up-and-coming Union general George B. McClellan,

John Pope, a former friend of Grant's in Mexico, had commanded Camp Yates but quit in disgust after being denied a promotion to brigadier general. Grant filled Pope's slot, which opened the door to additional opportunities. (loc)

**Note Grant's name first on the muster roll of the 21st Illinois Infantry. (isa)**

then serving Ohio. Still no luck. He tried the governor of Ohio, who had been a childhood friend. Nothing.

The *Galena Daily Gazette* rallied to his cause:

> *We are now in want of just such soldiers as he is, and we hope the government will invite him to higher command. He is the very soul of honor, and no man breathes who has a more patriotic heart. We want among our young soldiers the influence of the rare leadership of men like Captain Grant.*

Grant even sent a letter directly to the office of the adjutant general of the U.S. Army in Washington, D.C. "I have the honor, very respectfully, to render my services, until the close of the War, in such capacity as may be offered," he wrote. "[I]n view of my present age, and length of service, I feel myself competent to command a regiment," he wrote, "if the president, in his judgement, should see fit to entrust one to me."

The War Department never answered. Biographer Ronald White speculated that, "The harried [adjutant general, Lorenzo Thomas] must have put the request in a drawer, because fifteen years passed before it was discovered—in 1876—by a subsequent adjutant general."

During this period, Grant happened to be in St. Louis on the day newly raised Federal soldiers prevented a Confederate militia from taking control of the United States arsenal in the city. Grant called it "splendid work" that saved not just the arsenal but the city itself. "If St. Louis had been captured by the rebels it would have made a vast difference in our war," he later mused. "It would have been a terrible task to have recaptured St. Louis—one of the most difficult that could be given to any military man. Instead of a campaign before Vicksburg, it would have been a campaign before St. Louis."

Grant didn't realize it, but during this period of limbo, his own good work was actually catching up to him. One of the last regiments he'd mustered in, the 21st Illinois in Mattoon, was undergoing convulsions. Its colonel, a bombastic, hard-drinking rowdy named Simon S. Goode, had allowed discipline to slip so badly that men in the regiment raided local farms, caroused drunkenly, set fires, and rioted for bread. The junior officers petitioned Yates to replace Goode with Grant, who had made a deep impression on them during his brief time drilling them when they had mustered in. Yates followed their wishes and, on June 15, he telegraphed Grant to offer him the job.

*   *   *

When Grant showed up to take command of the regiment—a return to Camp Grant, as it happened—he arrived in "a plain blue blouse coat and an ordinary black felt hat, and never had about him a single mark to distinguish his rank." Two Illinois Congressmen who would go on to play major roles in Grant's military life greeted him. One was John McClernand, the other John Logan, who introduced Grant to the men with a two-hour speech. Concluding, he said, "Allow me to present you your new colonel, U. S. Grant."

Grant's first comments to the regiment, in a voice not loud but clear: "Men, go to your quarters."

And thus began Grant's effort to tame the untamed 21st. The regiment consisted of "lusty young men from the farms, shops, and offices of the district," said one writer. James L. Crane, who served as chaplain, described the regiment as "a sort of disorderly mass, a hodge-podge of entanglements, an unsystematic, unarranged hurly-burly of officers and privates."

"[John] Logan's popularity in this district was unbounded," Grant wrote of first meeting the man who would later become a trusted subordinate. Logan gave "a speech which he has hardly equaled since for force and eloquence. It breathed loyalty and devotion to the Union which inspired my men to such a point that they would have volunteered to remain in the army as long as an enemy of the country continued to bear arms against it." (loc)

**"[Grant] is no dissembler,** no assumer of snob dignity; he has more than ordinary freedom from selfishness, and appears to no one as an ambitious man. He is a sincere, thinking, real man; by real we mean that he does not take to shows, shams, or 'flourishes,' but to realities. . . .

"[H]e is magnanimous, having a special regard for the feelings and interests of others. He has no desire to rise by the fall of others; no glorying over another's abasement; no exulting over another's tears. . . ."

*– Chaplain James L. Crane, 21st Illinois*

Grant knew them from his days mustering them in and considered them good men overall, although as he later said, "There were men in it who could be led astray. . . ." He admitted, "I found it very hard work for a few days to bring all them into anything like subordination; but the good majority favored discipline, and by the application of a little regular army punishment all were reduced to as good discipline as one could ask."

Chaplain Crane spent considerable time with his new commander. "Grant would correct, and, if necessary, punish any want of conformity to rule, or neglect of orders, or infraction of regulation, in as cool and unruffled a manner as you would give directions to your gardener before breakfast," Crane observed. In less than ten days, Grant tamed the regiment. "All this complicated confusion was brought to order and subordination by his quiet, unostentatious vigor and vigilance," the chaplain added. The men began to call their commander "the quiet man."

Crane had heard the rumors from the prewar army that Grant was "a lover of ardent spirits" who "indulged too freely in their use," but he saw nothing of the sort. "I was with him for the most part of three months, in all sorts of weather, marches, and exposure," Crane wrote; "we ate at the same table, often slept in the same tent, and sat around the same camp-fire; and I never knew him to allow ardent spirits in the regiment, not did I ever know him to taste them in any form."

The men responded positively to Grant's firm but fair expectations, and Grant took notice. "I don't believe there is a more orderly set of troops in the volunteer service," he finally proclaimed. "I have been very strict with them and they seem to like it." And indeed, they did. "We knew we had a real soldier over us," one junior officer said approvingly. Chaplain Crane observed "a strong mutual attachment between Grant and the men of his regiment. . . ."

On July 3, orders came for the regiment to relocate to Quincy, Illinois, along the Mississippi River. Seeing an opportunity to continue their training on the march, Grant refused the opportunity to entrain them for a quicker ride. "I prefer to do my first marching in a friendly, and not in an enemy's, country," he told a superior. But en route, word arrived of a Federal regiment harried by Confederate troops on the Missouri side of the river, in Palmyra, so Grant rushed the 21st to the scene.

**Erected on July 11, 2008, at a cost of $2,950, a monument in Quincy, Illinois, marks the location where Grant's 21st Illinois crossed the Mississippi River to Palmyra, Missouri, on their first mission.** (js)

While that emergency quickly vanished, Grant's men kept busy with various duties but finally received orders to march toward the town of Florida. There, Confederate Col. Thomas Harris and a band of partisan rangers were harrying locals. The episode led to one of Grant's most important lessons of the war.

"[W]hen we got on the road and found every house deserted I was anything but easy," Grant later admitted. He maintained discipline, refusing any of his men to enter the abandoned homes. Eventually, the column neared a hill where Grant expected to find Harris's men waiting for them. "Harris had been encamped in a creek bottom for the sake of being near water," Grant explained. "The hills on either side of the creek extended to a considerable height, possibly more than a hundred feet." The position looked formidable.

"[M]y heart kept getting higher and higher until it felt to me as though it was in my throat," Grant said. "I would have given anything then to have been back in Illinois, but I did not have the moral courage to halt and consider what to do; I kept right on."

**Thomas Alexander Harris, sketched here for his April 1895 obituary in the Louisville, Kentucky, _Courier-Journal_, taught Grant one of Grant's most important lessons of the war—without even realizing it.** (cj)

In 1881, members of the 21st Illinois dedicated a monument in Ironton, Missouri's Emerson Park, commemorating the occasion of Grant's promotion to brigadier general. (isa)

Later in life, Grant saw something of himself in the early war troubles of Brig. Gen. Irvin McDowell, the Union general defeated at First Manassas. "You will remember people called him a drunkard and a traitor," Grant told a reporter. "Well, he never drank a drop of liquor in his life, and a more loyal man never lived." (loc)

The column crested the hill only to discover Harris's men had abandoned their camp.

"It occurred to me at once that Harris had been as much afraid of me as I had been of him," Grant realized. "This was a view of the question I had never taken before; but it was one I never forgot afterwards."

*    *    *

Upon the regiment's return from its illuminating mission, the men received several other assignments, most of which involved going from place to place in whack-a-mole fashion. But on August 5, Grant received the assignment that would finally propel him inexorably down the Mississippi River.

It was Chaplain Crane, newspaper in hand, who flagged him down. "Colonel, I have some news here that will interest you," he said.

"What have you, Chaplain?"

Crane passed him a copy of the *Missouri Daily Democrat*. "I see that you are made brigadier-general."

"Well, sir, I had no suspicion of it," Grant replied, taking a seat. "It never came from any request of mine. That's some of Washburne's work." President Lincoln had asked to the Congressional delegation for some recommendations for promotion, and Grant had unanimously been chosen as the first on a list of seven.

Grant's promotion came at a time of high tension for the Union. On July 21, just outside Manassas, Virginia, Confederate forces routed Federal forces in what became known as the battle of Bull Run. Then, on August 10, days after Grant's elevation, Federal forces lost a battle at Wilson's Creek near Springfield in southwest Missouri. The Federal commander, Brig. Gen. Nathaniel Lyon, fell as a casualty—the first general officer killed in the war. "I have a task before me of no trifling moment and want all the encouragement possible," he told Julia.

This image from *Frank Leslie's Illustrated Newspaper* shows the Union defeat at Wilson's Creek on August 10, 1861, which accentuated the state's already-tense situation. (loc)

Over the course of a few weeks, department commander Maj. Gen. John "The Pathfinder" Fremont shifted Grant from one posting to another across southern Missouri: Ironton, Jefferson City, Cape Girardeau. "My duties are active but I enjoy most excellent health," Grant wrote Julia.

Ultimately, Grant found himself in command of an area that encompassed southeast Missouri and southern Illinois: the river gateway of the Mississippi River to the Deep South. Grant's competence had impressed Fremont, who decided to place Grant at the tip of a spear Fremont was aiming down the Mississippi. "I believed him to be a man of great activity and promptness in obeying orders without question or hesitation," Fremont later explained. "I selected him for qualities I could not find combined in any other officer, for General Grant was a man of unassuming character, not given to self-elation, or dogged persistence, and of iron will." Coming from a man who personified self-elation and assuming character, this was high praise, indeed.

Grant's unflappable nature would prove vital for navigating a controversy that erupted soon after he arrived at his new posting.

John Fremont, the Republican Party's first presidential candidate, earned his nickname as "The Pathfinder" from his successful explorations of the American West. While press portrayals seemed romanticized, Fremont actually thought of himself in such inflated terms. (loc)

*Belmont*

# CHAPTER TWO
*September–November 1861*

Grant's first major victory came without firing a shot, yet the ramifications became huge.

On September 4, Confederate Maj. Gen. Leonidus Polk moved forces into western Kentucky to occupy the town of Columbus, which sat on a high bluff overlooking the Mississippi River. Control of the town helped secure Confederate control of the river.

Grant recieved intelligence—flawed, as it turned out—that Polk looked to further consolidate his position by moving on the larger town of Paducah to the northeast. Paducah sat at the confluence of the Ohio and Tennessee rivers, and the Cumberland River emptied into the Ohio just a few miles upriver. Paducah, then, could serve as a choke point for traffic along the Ohio—a potentially crippling blow to any northern commerce that depended on the river.

However, Kentucky had formally declared its neutrality, which Polk's presence violated.

Grant, newly minted as a brigadier general, had encamped at Cairo, Illinois, at the confluence of the Ohio and Mississippi. "Cairo does not appear to be particularly sickly at this time," he reported to Julia. "It is usually considered to be an unhealthy place and looks as if it must be so. The ground is on a level

**Steam transportation made it possible for Grant to shift troops quickly within his department. His understanding of the rivers and how to use them would prove an instrumental element of his success in the west.** (loc)

with the river at ordinary stage and much below it at high water." Julia, who soon joined him there, was shocked by "how angry the river was and how desolate Cairo seemed."

**A small park near Paducah's convention center contains several historical markers that address the city's Civil War history, including Grant's occupation.** (cm)

Paducah sat to Cairo's northeast, potentially outflanking the Federal base. Grant alerted his commander, Fremont, to the danger, but then moved on his own initiative to occupy the town. "It was the work of only a few hours to get the boats manned, with coal aboard and steam up," Grant recalled.

Federals arrived in Paducah on September 6, beating some 4,000 Confederates by no more than six or eight hours. "When the National troops entered the town the citizens were taken by surprise," Grant noted. "I never after saw such consternation depicted on the faces of the people." Paducahians expected Polk and had festooned the streets with Confederate flags. Grant pretended not to notice—but he replaced the secessionist flags with flags of the United States.

"I have come among you, not as an enemy, but as your friend and fellow-citizen," he announced,

> not to injure or annoy you, but to respect the rights, and to defend and enforce the rights of all loyal citizens. An enemy, in rebellion against our common government, has taken possession of, and planted its guns upon the soil of Kentucky and fired upon our flag. . . . He is moving upon your city. I am here to defend you against this enemy and to assert and maintain the authority and sovereignty to your Government and mine. . . . I shall deal only with armed rebellion and its aiders and abetors. You can pursue your usual avocations without fear or hindrance.

Having made his point, Grant returned to his headquarters almost at once. "On my return to Cairo I found my authorization from department headquarters for me to take Paducah 'if I felt strong enough,'" he later revealed. But soon thereafter, Fremont sent a reprimand to his proactive subordinate. When Grant had made his move on Paducah, he informed the Kentucky legislature about what he was up to out of an abundance of caution not to seem too aggressive against the state's neutrality. Fremont, ever the politician, objected to Grant getting anywhere near politics himself.

President Lincoln—who thought the Bluegrass State so important that he once said, "I hope to have God on my side, but I must have Kentucky"—read the overall situation differently. He didn't know Grant except through Washburne's advocacy. Reading Grant's "Address to the Citizens of Paducah" created a strong favorable impression. "The modesty and brevity of that address shows that the officer issuing it understands the situation and is a proper man to command there at the time," he said.

The Kentucky legislature formally approved of Grant's action and became increasingly hostile toward Confederate influences. Thanks to Polk's missteps and Grant's prompt exploitation of the situation, Lincoln would "have" the state in the end.

\* \* \*

"From the occupation of Paducah up to the early part of November nothing important occurred with the troops under my command . . ." Grant later summarized. "They were growing impatient lying idle so long, almost in hearing of the guns of the enemy they had volunteered to fight against."

In early November, Grant received orders from the Pathfinder to conduct a demonstration against Polk's forces still in the Bluegrass State. Grant was to move southward from Cairo toward Columbus, Kentucky, on the east bank of the Mississippi and Belmont, Missouri, on the west bank. Grant considered demonstrations a waste of time and resources, but he complied. This demonstration would bear unexpected benefits for Grant.

At Belmont, Confederates had established Camp Johnston, a large training camp from which they were

According to Grant's son, Fred, this photo "was taken in Cairo, Ill., in 1861, and is a remarkably good picture of General Grant as he looked at that time. He had always worn his beard trimmed short until he was appointed colonel of the 21st Illinois; but during the time that he was serving in Missouri he did not trim his beard, nor did he do so on being stationed at Cairo after his appointment as brigadier-general. After he had fought the battle of Belmont, he sent for his family to come on from Galena and make him a visit. This picture had been taken just before the visit, and one of the first things that my mother said to him was, that she did not like the length of his beard." Grant shaved the beard shortly thereafter and grew back a shorter one. (b&l)

preparing to go into western Missouri. Grant had previously sent a 3,000-man task force into the state under Col. Richard Oglesby, and any Confederate incursion would cut them off. For that reason, Grant focused his demonstration on the Missouri side of the river.

Grant messaged St. Louis, telling Fremont that unless he heard orders to the contrary, he would attack. No such orders came and, having no orders to the contrary, Grant and his 3,100 soldiers attacked the 5,000 Confederate soldiers encamped at Belmont on the morning of November 7.

The attack turned into a surprisingly stout four-hour fight. Confederates eventually withdrew toward the far side of the river, and Grant's forces occupied the camp. However, heady with success, the men seemed to lose self-control. "At this point they became demoralized from their victory and failed to reap its full reward," Grant later lamented. Rather than finish off the retreating Confederates, Grant's undisciplined men began to loot the camp. Officers not only failed to bring order, they joined in the looting. Unable to bring order himself, Grant ordered the tents set afire, which seemed to focus his men.

The respite gave Grant the opportunity to point out the riverboats full of Confederates crossing from the Kentucky bank, and they began to land between Grant's army and the army's own small flotilla. Panic soon set in, and some men began to talk of surrender. However, Grant calmly announced, "we

**Henry Walke, commander of the *Tyler*, sketched the re-embarkation of Grant's men onto their transports after the battle.** (b&l)

had cut our way in and could cut our way out just as well," which seemed a "new revelation to the officers and soldiers."

The men formed up quickly, and Grant called the Chicago Light Battery into action, ordering them to double-shot their guns with canister. Their heavy fire opened a gap in the Confederate line, widened by Col. John "Black Jack" Logan's 31st Illinois, which rushed through. Caught off guard by the Federal bravado, Confederates fell back even further, widening the gap in their line and allowing Grant's men to reach their boats.

Grant then remembered a regiment, the 27th Illinois, that he had sent on detached detail south of the camp to protect the small army's flank. They had not been informed of the turn of events. During the battle, Grant had his horse shot out from underneath him, but now a cooperative lieutenant offered him a replacement mount. Grant put spurs to the horse and galloped to them.

But when he reached the position where the regiment should have been, they were gone. They had withdrawn to the boats, without orders, when they saw the main body of troops falling back. Grant now abruptly found himself in the precarious position with the rebels between him and the river. Slowly, so as to

As a politician, John McClernand had speechified on Grant's behalf to new recruits. Soon thereafter, McClernand's relationship with President Lincoln netted him a commission, and he soon found himself serving under Grant. McClernand made himself indispensable during the mission to Paducah. "I must acknowledge my obligations to General McClernand, commanding this force, for the active and efficient cooperation exhibited by him in fitting out the expedition," Grant wrote. Over the months that followed, though, the relationship between the two men would curdle considerably. (loc)

not attract attention to himself, Grant rode his horse through a not-yet-cleared cornfield. He wore an old infantry greatcoat of faded blue and hoped that he looked like an enlisted man. Nevertheless, two Rebel officers spotted him. "Look there!" one of them yelled to their men. "Yonder goes a Yankee officer. Practice your marksmanship on him." Remarkably, though Grant was no more than 50 yards away, not one man raised his weapon to fire.

Grant galloped to the river. It had been the driest summer in memory, so the Mississippi River was low with a steep drop from the bank. Grant saw the boats were pulling away, but the commander of Grant's command boat, *Belle Memphis* saw him. Although the captain did not come back to the bank, he did cut his engines. "My horse put his fore feet over the bank without hesitation or urging, and with his hind feet well under him, slid down the bank and trotted aboard the boat . . . over a single gang plank," Grant recounted.

As the boat pulled away into the river, Grant climbed up to the captain's cabin behind the pilot house to lie down, exhausted from the day's stresses. But soon, he heard sporadic firing going on outside and went on deck to investigate. Confederates above them on the riverbank were offering parting shots, and some of Grant's men were returning the favor, although the Federals had clearly steamed out of range. Grant ordered them to stop, then returned to the cabin.

Inside, he noticed a bullet hole in the bulkhead where his head would have been had he stayed on the sofa and not gone out to investigate.

John McClernand parlayed his political relationship with President Lincoln into a senior field command. Grant would, in turn, demonstrate political adeptness of his own, effectively navigating the tangle presented by that relationship. Here, McClernand (right) is pictured with Lincoln and detective Alan Pinkerton near the Antietam battlefield in October 1862, shortly after the battle of Belmont. (loc)

**On the day of the battle of Belmont,** Julia Grant had a mid-afternoon premonition. She was in the midst of preparation to join Grant in Cairo but suddenly "felt nervous." "I went to my room to rest for a few moments, when I distinctly saw Ulys a few rods from me," she recounted. "I only saw his head and shoulders, about as high as if he were on horseback. He looked at me so earnestly and, I thought, so reproachfully that I started up and said, 'Ulys!' . . . I started that evening with my little ones. We heard of the battle of Belmont, however, before we left. Ulys met me almost before the train stopped. I told him of my seeing him on the day of the battle. He asked at what hour, and when I told him, he said, 'That is singular. Just about that time I was on horseback and in great peril, and I thought of you and the children and what would become of you if I were lost. I was thinking of you, my dear Julia, and very earnestly, too."

As the small army steamed north, they found the missing regiment of Illinoisians and swung to the bank to pick them up. Everyone thereafter safely returned to Cairo. Of the 3,100 men Grant took into battle, he lost 607; Confederates lost 641 killed, wounded, or missing from the 5,000 men engaged.

Critics blamed Grant for a loss—he had, after all, been driven from the battlefield by a superior force—but time soon vindicated Grant's action. "The two objects for which the battle of Belmont was fought were fully accomplished," he later pointed out. "The enemy gave up all idea of detaching troops from Columbus. His losses were very heavy for that period of the war."

On a tactical level, Grant's men were bloodied at Belmont for the first time. The small battle gave them a much-needed morale boost and did much to de-mystify and de-romanticize war for them. That "confidence in themselves . . . did not desert them through the war," Grant proudly noted.

Perhaps most importantly, far away in Washington, D.C., Lincoln heard Grant's name again—and again in a favorable light. Grant's second in command, Brig. Gen. John McClernand, was an Illinois politician with Lincoln's ear, and the self-promoting McClernand made sure to crow about the victory at Belmont because doing so made him look good. Grant would benefit from McClernand's efforts, although the two would not be on such mutually beneficial terms for long.

# Forts Henry and Donelson

## CHAPTER THREE
*February 1862*

Known as "Old Brains" for his bookish brilliance on military matters, Henry Halleck originally rose to prominence in the wartime army upon the recommendation of General in Chief Winfield Scott. When John Fremont's progressive views on slavery made him a political liability in border-state Missouri, Lincoln shuffled the Pathfinder to a quieter front in the mountains of western Virginia and placed Halleck in departmental command along the upper Mississippi. It would prove a consequential pick for Grant.

In the weeks after Belmont, Grant's men "did little but prepare for the long struggle which proved to be before them," yet Grant eagerly sought an opportunity to *do* something. Then, in early January, an expedition into western Kentucky sparked an idea: a Confederate fort on the Tennessee River, Fort Henry, looked vulnerable. Grant knew Halleck "but very slightly" but hoped his new commander would let him try and take the fort.

Grant asked permission to go to St. Louis to meet with Halleck personally to put his idea before him. Halleck reluctantly gave him an audience but cut Grant short before Grant had even "uttered many sentences . . . as if my plan was preposterous," Grant

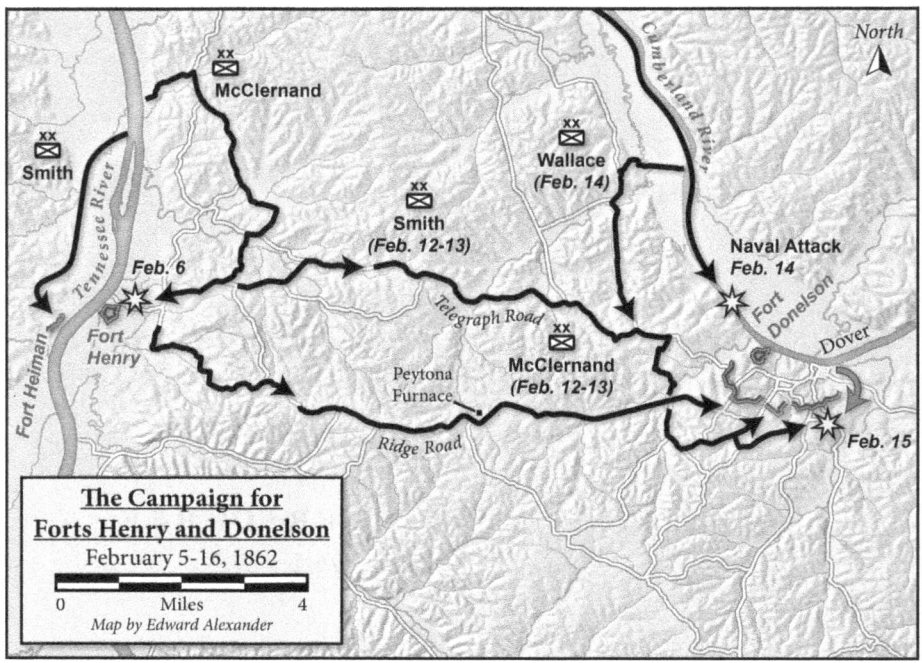

**THE CAMPAIGN FOR FORTS HENRY AND DONELSON, FEBRUARY 5–16, 1862**—After landing upriver of Fort Henry, Grant's men arrived after the fort's capitulation. Grant then directed them eastward toward Fort Donelson and laid siege.

Grant's successful partnership with Andrew Hull Foote served as a template for Grant's later army-navy operations. (loc)

recalled. Halleck dismissed him with a stringing *No.* "I returned to Cairo very much crestfallen," the dejected subordinate admitted.

Undeterred, Grant began talking about his idea with Flag Officer Andrew Hull Foote, commander of the Mississippi River Squadron. Foote liked it and asked Secretary of the Navy Gideon Welles for support. Foote intervened with Halleck, who approved it because Foote had joined in.

Grant and Foote developed a joint Army/Navy operation in which Grant would circle around Fort Henry and assault from the land side while Foote bombarded the fort from the water. However, heavy rains helped the navy and hindered the army.

Confederates had placed Fort Henry poorly, at the water level, and because of the rain, it was under a couple of feet of water when Foote steamed up and opened fire. The bombardment lasted about an hour before the flooded fort capitulated. Foote sent a rowboat into the fort to pick up the surrendering officers and 90 men.

The navy and Mother Nature subdued Fort Henry before Grant's army even got into the fight. (loc)

That same rain created deep mud that delayed Grant's movement. The naval assault had finished before the army got anywhere near the place for its assault. Undisturbed that he'd missed the action, Grant congratulated Foote on the naval victory.

Grant reported that Fort Henry had fallen, and he would move on to Fort Donelson in two days. He didn't. "The rain continued to fall so heavily that the roads became impassable for artillery and wagon trains," Grant explained.

Donelson sat 12 miles due east of Henry, situated on the Cumberland River. Getting the men and supplies ready for the march took longer than Grant planned because of the muddy roads and poor weather.

On February 12, Grant's army of some 15,000 men finally set out on two parallel roads. He felt a mixture of confidence in his plan and contempt for the opposing commanders. "I had known General [Gideon] Pillow in Mexico, and judged that with any force, no matter how small I could march up to within gunshot of any intrenchments he was given to hold," Grant later said. "I knew that [John] Floyd was in command, but he was no soldier. . . ."

No sooner did Grant's army set out than the weather played another trick. The sudden appearance

Grant described Fort Donelson in his memoirs: "The fort stood on high ground, some of it as much as a hundred feet above the Cumberland. Strong protection to the heavy guns in the water batteries had been obtained by cutting away places for them in the bluff. To the west there was a line of rifle-pits some two miles back from the river at the farthest point. This line ran generally along the crest of high ground, but in one place crossed a ravine which opens into the river between the village and the fort. The ground inside and outside of this intrenched line was very broken and generally wooded. The trees outside of the rifle-pits had been cut down for a considerable way out, and had been felled so that their tops lay outwards from the intrenchments. The limbs had been trimmed and pointed, and thus formed an abatis in front of the greater part of the line." (us)

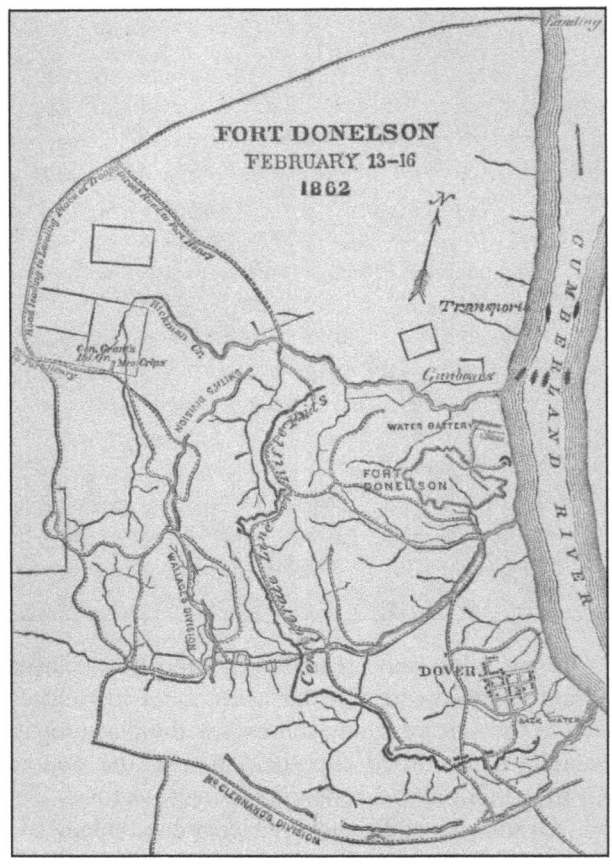

of warm, spring-like weather inspired the men to shed their overcoats as they marched. They soon began to store them, along with their blankets, along the side of the roads.

Meanwhile, Flag Officer Foote steamed downriver from the Tennessee to the Ohio, then upriver to the Cumberland, so he could provide naval support for Grant. He had hoped to repeat his easy victory at Fort Henry, but he soon discovered Fort Donelson was an entirely different situation. The fort was strategically placed on a high, sloping bank at a curve in the river, with heavy guns sighted down the bowling alley-like Cumberland. Upper and Lower Water Batteries—some 12 guns in all—could deliver an accurate and devastating fire at any approaching ships, which would have to struggle against the current in any attempt to close with the fort.

As February 12th turned to the 13th, Grant struggled to get in place on the hills and sharply rolling land around the outer lines of Fort Donelson even as Foote prepared to move against its river side. Grant's troops sparred with Confederates along the lines as each side probed the other to determine strength and position, but no major fighting broke out.

By the end of the day on February 13, two significant features began falling at the same time: night and snow. A bitterly cold winter storm had settled in over the area, and temperatures plummeted as darkness fell. Snow turned into freezing rain, then sleet, then back into heavy snow. Temperatures dropped below zero.

The troops were miserable and vainly wished they had those greatcoats and blankets they had put aside. They had only their uniforms to keep them warm, but those quickly became soaked in the wintery mix. Colonel Richard Oglesby of the 8th Illinois called it "one of the most persecuting snow storms ever known to this country." To make matters worse, orders prohibited campfires because the army's position was much too close to the Confederates, who also went without fires. As the night and darkness deepened, the misery of both sides worsened to agony. By daybreak, men were "nearly torpid from the intense cold."

Early in the afternoon of February 14, the thin, black double plumes of the navy's seven-boat armada steamed around the sharp bend of the Cumberland a half mile from Fort Donelson—and in clear view of the looming heavy guns. In the exchange of "iron valentines," the water batteries wreaked devastating damage on the naval fleet, which had to withdraw downriver.

The repulse proved a pivotal moment for Grant, although no one realized it at the moment. "Some of the gunboats were to run the batteries, get above the fort and above the village of Dover," he later

**Had the navy successfully run Fort Donelson's guns and landed troops downriver of the fort, Confederate defenses would have been breached. Would subsequent events have even offered an opportunity for the kind of "unconditional surrender" that gave Grant his famous nickname?** (cm)

Charles Francis Smith had been commandant of cadets at West Point when Grant was a student there. Grant referred to him as "a most accomplished soldier" and was a little starstruck having Smith serve as a subordinate. "General," Smith told Grant, "I am now a subordinate. I know a soldier's duty. Pray, feel no awkwardness whatever about our new relations." (loc)

explained. Had they done so, and then forced the capitulation of the fort, the career-defining event that followed may have never taken place at all.

In the very early hours of February 15, Foote called Grant to meet with him on his flagship, anchored some seven miles away, to discuss next steps. "Will you do me the favor to come on board at your earliest convenience, as I am disabled from walking by a contusion and cannot possibly get to see you," Foote said apologetically. Grant answered the summons, but the intense cold had frozen the ground solid. "This made travel on horseback even slower than through the mud," Grant recounted, "but I went as fast as the roads would allow."

Grant left orders not to bring on an engagement with the enemy. There had been low-level skirmishing between the two armies—mostly brought on by McClernand disobeying orders—but Grant did not want a battle to break out while he was away meeting with Foote. Unfortunately for his army, he did not leave someone in command when he left. "I had no idea that there would be any engagement on land unless I brought it on myself," he admitted. It was a costly mistake that nearly lost the battle and his career.

Grant met with Foote, who offered him a good cigar and told him that he was going to have to withdraw to Cairo for repairs and refitting for his boat, which had taken a terrible beating. He expected to be gone a month or so.

Grant's heart sank with that news. He didn't want to be hunkered down around Fort Donelson for a month, but he did not feel he could successfully take the fort without the navy's help. He asked Foote to leave a boat or two just around the bend in the Cumberland River, with steam up, to make Confederates think they were just out of sight and planning a return assault. At the very least, that would maintain morale within Grant's army. Foote agreed.

Grant left the meeting thinking he was going to have to begin siege operations while he awaited the navy's return. "But the enemy relieved me from this necessity," he discovered.

Aides waited on the riverbank with news that a battle had erupted in Grant's absence. Confederates had broken out of their lines and attacked

McClernand's troops and driven them back a mile or more. The situation looked desperate for the Federals, made worse because there was no plan to meet an attempted break-out and no one possessed command authority to take control and fight back. Finally, Brig. Gen. Lew Wallace had taken it upon himself, without orders, to intervene. Wallace's last-minute effort had helped to save the day.

A seven-mile ride over treacherous roads brought Grant to the scene of the breakthrough. "I saw the men standing in knots talking in the most excited manner," he recalled. "No officer seemed to be giving any directions. The soldiers had their muskets, but no ammunition, while there were tons at hand."

Pointing to the ammunition crates scattered about the area, he ordered his aides to tell the men to open the boxes and rearm. Then he immediately ordered that they retake the lost ground. Grant's directive "acted like a charm." The men, he later said, "only wanted someone to give them a command."

Grant then rode to the other parts of the battlefield, ordering his aides not to gallop but trot their horses to keep Confederates from thinking they were panicked, which might encourage them to attack all the harder.

Soldiers told Grant that the dead and captured Confederates carried full backpacks. "[H]e has attempted to force his way out," Grant realized. "Some of our men are pretty badly demoralized, but the enemy must be more so. . . . [T]he one who attacks first now will be victorious. . . ." Grant determined to make an immediate assault on the opposite end of the line. "[T]he enemy will have to be in a hurry if he gets ahead of me," he concluded.

Brigadier General C. F. Smith's counterattack against Brig. Gen. Simon Buckner's lines on the Confederate right proved successful. Coupled with Wallace's counterattack on the Confederate left and Grant's subsequent rally, the initial Confederate success reversed entirely. "There was now no doubt but that the Confederates must surrender or be captured the next day," Grant declared.

Floyd and Pillow, as senior commanders, were unwilling to bear the responsibility of surrendering. They instead slunk away in the night, foisting the

Sitting along the banks of the Cumberland River, the Dover Hotel served as the location for surrender negotiations between Grant and Buckner. (cm)

Grant was surprised Gideon Pillow, commander of the fort, had not surrendered it. "Well," Simon Buckner told him, "he thought you would rather have hold of him than any other man in the Southern Confederacy." Grant replied wryly, "Oh, no. If I had got him, I'd have let him go again; he will do us more good commanding you fellows." (vmhc)

unpleasant task upon Buckner, who was third in command, "but much the most capable soldier," according to Grant.

At the end of the day's fighting, Grant had retired to his headquarters at the cabin of the Widow Crisp. Before daylight on February 16, C. F. Smith brought a message from the fort that had come through the line: Buckner wanted to appoint commissioners to negotiate surrender terms.

"What answer shall I send to this?" Grant asked his former mentor.

"Bah!" Smith barked. "No terms to the damned rebels but unconditional surrender!"

That sounded good to Grant. He sat at a small kitchen table and asked for pencil and paper. His three-sentence reply acknowledged receipt of Buckner's message, then said, "No terms except an unconditional and immediate surrender can be accepted. I propose to move immediately upon your works."

Grant passed the note to Smith for delivery. "General," he said, "I guess this will do."

"It could not be better," Smith replied.

Buckner, an old friend and West Point classmate, thought otherwise. He called them "Unchivalrous terms"—but accepted them.

Buckner and Grant soon met in the Dover Hotel on the banks of the Cumberland River, where Buckner surrendered his army of more than 13,000 men, artillery, and cavalry. "If I had been in command, you would not have gotten Donelson as easily as you did," Buckner told his old friend.

"If you had been in command, I should not have tried in the way I did," Grant admitted. Overall, the two old friends had a "very friendly" conversation, despite the circumstances.

The United States army had won its first major victory of the war, taking an entire Confederate army, along with its artillery, out of the war. Moreover, the fort's fall opened the Cumberland River all the way to Nashville, which immediately posed a tempting target.

Grant, meanwhile, became the darling of the nation, hailed as a hero. His image appeared on newspaper front-pages across the country. Drawing from Grant's message to Buckner, the public recast his initials, U. S., as "Unconditional Surrender"—a nickname that seemed nearly providential.

President Lincoln immediately rewarded Grant with a promotion to major general. Less than a year earlier, Grant had been a civilian desperately trying to get into the war; now he was a two-star commander of an army.

But as Grant would soon discover, not everyone was pleased by his success.

**When Americans first met the hero of Fort Donelson in the newspapers, they met the long-bearded version. Grant had, by then, reverted back to his shorter beard on Julia's orders.** (hw)

*Intrigues*

## CHAPTER FOUR

*February–March 1862*

Following the fall of the forts, Grant wanted to keep moving, which was to become his hallmark trait. He advocated moving immediately upon Nashville and taking the mountains of war supplies stockpiled there before Confederates could evacuate them. Grant telegraphed Halleck that, unless he received orders *not* to go there, he would travel to Nashville to talk with Brig. Gen. Don Carlos Buell, commander of the Army of the Ohio.

As it happened, Buell's army, on the other side of Nashville, was well positioned to march in and snatch the Confederate supplies—but Buell didn't want to take the city because crossing the Cumberland River would have put him in Grant's district and under Grant's command, which was distasteful to him because he had outranked Grant on the old army. So, he dallied and lost the supplies to Confederate Col. Nathan Bedford Forrest, who had escaped with his cavalry from Fort Donelson rather than needlessly surrender. The city eventually surrendered on February 25, 1862.

As the first Confederate state capital to fall, the loss of Nashville dealt a serious blow to Confederate morale. Equally important, the city gave the Federal

**What should have been a time of triumph morphed into a blurry time of confusion for Grant in the wake of Fort Donelson.** (ac/cf)

war effort a major distribution point for men and materials to move throughout the Western Theater.

**The fall of Nashville changed the strategic situation in the Western Theater for the rest of the war.** (cm)

"Events have cast on our arms and hopes the gloomiest of shadows," Confederate President Jefferson Davis lamented.

Unbeknownst to Grant, Halleck, or the War Department, during this period, a rebel telegrapher had gotten into position to intercept Grant's telegrams. Grant thought his response to requests and his routinely required reports were all going through when, in fact, they were not. "Why do you not obey my orders?" a flabbergasted Halleck demanded of him.

The spy "deserted his post after a short time and went south taking his dispatches with him," Grant later learned, but in the meantime, the glitch in communication provided Henry Halleck with a useful opportunity for intrigue.

Neither Halleck nor his superior, Federal General-in-Chief George McClellan, had much favor for Grant. Jealous that Grant's star was ascending, Halleck told McClellan that he "could get nothing out of [Grant]," that Grant had gone to Nashville, beyond the limits of his command, without Halleck's authority, and that the Army of the Tennessee "was more demoralized by victory that the army at Bull Run had been by defeat."

In a follow-up, Halleck intimated that Grant was "up to his old habits," implying that Grant was in the bottle and irresponsible. "It is hard to censure a successful general immediately after a victory, but I think he richly deserves it," Halleck said.

While the charges were all untrue, McClellan didn't know it. "The future success of our cause demands that proceedings such as Grant's should at once be checked," he replied. "Do not hesitate to arrest him at once if the good of the service requires it." McClellan urged Halleck to consider his note "a positive order" if it smoothed the way.

Ironically, as these intrigues unfolded, Grant continued to show faith in both Halleck and McClellan. In a letter to Julia, Grant said of Halleck, "I regard him as one of the greatest men of the age and there are not two men in the United States who I would prefer serving under to McClellan & Halleck. They would be my own choice for the positions they fill if left to me to make."

Upon Grant's return to his temporary headquarters in Clarksville, Tennessee, Halleck telegraphed him to put Brig. Gen. C. F. Smith in charge of the Army of the Tennessee for its next mission while Grant was to stay at his headquarters.

Smith took the army down the Tennessee River to Pittsburg Landing, nearly to the Mississippi state line. From there, the army would set forth on an expedition to the rail crossroads at Corinth, Mississippi, where the Memphis and Charleston Railroad intersected with the Mobile and Ohio Railroad. The east-west Memphis and Charleston connected the Mississippi River with the Atlantic Ocean, while the north-south Mobile and Ohio connected the Gulf of Mexico with the Mississippi River at Columbus, Kentucky. The strategic importance of the railroad made the little village of Corinth a place of great interest to both armies.

**Throughout the war, Grant was keenly aware of the benefits—and restrictions—the telegraph could offer. He looked at the telegraph as a tether, but did his best work "off leash" and took operational advantage of the leeway such freedom offered. After a Confederate sympathizer interfered with Grant's telecommunications in February 1862, Grant appointed a personal telegrapher, Samuel Beckwith, to personally handle all correspondence. Beckwith became known as "Grant's Shadow." (b&l)**

Henry Halleck would prove a long-standing thorn in Grant's side, although he went to great lengths to conceal his role in Grant's troubles. "I never knew the truth," Grant admitted, "until General [Adam] Badeau unearthed the facts in his researches for his history of my campaigns," published in 1881. (loc)

Grant, meanwhile, waited in limbo, puzzled and angry about the rug being jerked out from under him for no visible reason. He had gone from a national hero "in less than three weeks," to someone "virtually in arrest and without a command," he lamented. What had happened?

As Halleck tersely explained, "Your going to Nashville without authority, and when your presence with your troops was of the utmost importance, was a matter of very serious complaint in Washington, so much so that I was advised to arrest you on your return."

Grant began filing repeated requests for Halleck to relieve him of command so an inquiry into the matter could be conducted to clear him. Meanwhile, in Washington, Elihu Washburne—Grant's Galena congressman and ardent champion—had heard about the lowdown dealings with Grant. He even caught wind that Grant was apparently about to be court-martialed out of the army. Washburne went to Lincoln, an old and close friend from back in the days when they both served in the Illinois State House, and told him about the situation.

Lincoln was shocked. *Wire Halleck about the matter*, he told Secretary of War Stanton, *and ask him, specifically: What did Grant do?*

Lincoln wanted an inquiry into any charges; otherwise, he wanted Grant restored to command. "I can't spare this man," Lincoln reportedly said. "He fights." Grant scholar Brooks Simpson has determined this statement is probably apocryphal. Even so, it continues to hold sway in Grant lore because it illustrates the support Lincoln eventually developed for him as a general willing to take the fight to the enemy at a time when so few others took similar initiative.

Realizing his efforts to replace Grant and remove a potential rival were not going to work, Halleck had already decided to reinstate Grant to command of the Army of the Tennessee. Nevertheless, the telegram from Adjutant General Lorenzo Thomas— by direction of Lincoln and Stanton—must have been quite a shock to Halleck, who was unaware that Grant had connections that apparently went all the way to the executive mansion. Lincoln had seen through the subterfuge and caught Halleck in his plot to ruin Grant.

On March 13, Halleck wired Grant, telling him that all charges had been resolved and that he was to join the army at Savannah, Tennessee. "Instead of relieving you," he said, "I wish you, as soon as your new army is in the field, to assume immediate command, and lead it to new victories."

At no point did Halleck's duplicity or dis-ingenuousness come to light. "I felt very grateful to him, and supposed it was his interposition that had set me right with the government . . ." Grant wrote years later in his memoirs. "[H]e did not inform me that it was his own reports that had created all the trouble."

"[George] McClellan to me is one of the mysteries of the war," Grant said. "He had the way of inspiring you with the idea of immense capacity, if he would only have a chance." (loc)

*Shiloh*

## CHAPTER FIVE
*April 1862*

On March 17, Grant arrived in Savannah, Tennessee, where he set up headquarters at the Cherry Mansion. General C. F. Smith—in command of the army in his stead—had established headquarters there, and Grant saw no need to change the location. However, what Grant found there bothered him.

First, he discovered Smith seriously ill from an injury to his leg. Smith had stepped from boat to boat at Pittsburg Landing, and they had pushed apart, causing him to fall against one and scrape one of his shins from ankle to knee. The injury had become infected and was curdling into blood poisoning. He would die from the wound a few days after the battle of Shiloh.

Second, half of the army was around the small town of Savannah while the other was at Pittsburg Landing, eight miles south of the town. Being strung out between the two points was of great concern to Grant, who determined to bring the halves together as soon as possible.

To make the problem worse, Grant had to wait for Maj. Gen. Don Carlos Buell to march his Army of the Ohio from Columbia, Tennessee, south of Nashville, and join the Army of the Tennessee before

The Cherry Mansion in Savannah, Tennessee, heard not only the clomping of Grant's boots but the clunk of his crutch—an unwanted accessory picked up following a horseback riding accident. (ac/cf)

The Cherry Mansion in Savannah, Tennessee, overlooked the Tennessee River, which flows through town south to north. The trip to Pittsburg Landing, therefore, was a slow one because boats had to power against the current all the way to the landing. (loc)

the combined forces could march on Corinth. Grant chafed at the wait: he knew Buell was in no hurry to join him because Buell didn't want to be under Grant's command. Waiting for something or someone was not something Grant did easily. He was eager to move on Albert Sidney Johnston and engage him.

During this period, Grant maintained his Cherry Mansion headquarters so he could meet Buell as soon as Buell arrived in Savannah. He settled into the routine of sailing up the Tennessee River daily to Pittsburg Landing, receiving recruits and assigning them to units, and training men on the open fields around the landing. He had some 37,000 men, most of whom had never "seen the elephant." Many didn't even know how to fire a gun. Each evening, he would return to Savannah.

Maj. Gen. Don Carlos Buell suffered from the same intense cautiousness as his friend, George McClellan, whom he addressed as "Dear Friend" in correspondence. Grant biographer Ron White writes that Grant and Buell operated "on different understandings of the military strategy required in Tennessee," which frustrated the more active-minded Grant. (loc)

Worried that the supply depot at Crump's Landing, five miles north of Pittsburg Landing, might be the target of a Confederate attack, Grant stationed Maj. Gen. Lew Wallace there with 5,000 troops. Grant worked out a plan that, if Confederates attacked Pittsburg Landing, Wallace would march his troops to the fight by the shortest route, the river road running beside the Tennessee River. To make the trip faster, scouts also developed an alternative route, one that curved away from the river and came back to Pittsburg Landing from the west along a new road and a bridge across Owl Creek.

Grant paid less attention to his defenses around Pittsburg Landing, instead prioritizing the training his men needed. Later, armchair generals would

levy heavy criticism at him for it. "I regarded the campaign we were engaged in as an offensive one," he would explain, "and had no idea that the enemy would leave strong intrenchment to take the initiative when he knew he would be attacked where he was if he remained." He also believed the terrain around the landing was so broken with wooded areas, open spaces, and deep ravines that any trenches would need to be behind the troops and would do no good.

Named for local tavern owner "Pitts" Tucker, Pittsburg Landing provided convenient access to the Tennessee River in an area with otherwise-high banks. On the opposite bank of the river, a road ran northeast to Savannah. (loc)

Another issue Grant took into consideration when deciding not to dig trenches was his worry that the men would interpret it as an act of cowardice, or "showing the white feather." The war was only 51 weeks old, and no battle the size of the one about to erupt had yet been fought. The inexperienced men—not yet veteran fighters—felt that honorable men did not hide behind trees or breastworks. "Real men," they believed, stood and faced the foe and gave measure for measure. It would take the battle of Shiloh to change that.

On April 4, Grant experienced yet one more misfortune. "The night was one of impenetrable darkness, with rain pouring down in torrents; nothing was visible to the eye, except as revealed by the frequent flashes of lightning . . ." Grant recounted. "[M]y horse's feet slipped under him, and he fell with my leg under his body. The extreme softness of the ground, from the excessive rains of the few preceding days, no doubt saved me from a severe injury and protracted lameness. As it was, my ankle was very much injured, so much so that my boot had to be cut off. For two or three days after I was unable to walk except with crutches."

\*   \*   \*

Grant forever denied that Confederates surprised him at Shiloh, but the opening engagement in Fraley Field—where Federals went out to investigate reports of unexpected strange noises—demonstrated otherwise. (cm)

As Grant dealt with his injured leg that Friday night, 44,000 Confederates were already advancing on the Army of the Tennessee. They had set out from Corinth, Mississippi, on April 2 on a 20-mile march that would bring them to Pittsburg Landing, intent on catching Grant and his Federals by surprise and destroying the Yankee threat.

Their commander, Gen. Albert Sidney Johnston, had been considered one of the foremost soldiers in the South, but early Confederate strategy had hampered his efforts, and then the loss of forts Henry and Donelson—under his overall if not direct control—had badly damaged his reputation. The complaints had grown so loud that Confederate President Jefferson Davis exclaimed, "If General Johnston is not a General, then we have no General!"

Reports had tipped Johnston to Buell's approach, and he decided to take the fight to Grant before Buell could reinforce him. That would eliminate the strongest Federal threat in the Western Theater and restore Johnston's reputation.

Johnston had hoped to attack on April 4, but poor roads and inexperienced troops made for slow progress. Not until the morning of April 6, around 5:00 a.m., did he finally launch his assault. The initial onslaught favored the Confederates. Confident of victory, he predicted his army would water its horses in the Tennessee River that night.

Grant started that morning gingerly, hobbling down the steep hallway steps from his second-floor bedroom to the Cherry Mansion's dining room. He was gently using a crutch, moving carefully so as to not hurt his already injured left foot and leg. Passing the crutch to an aide, he eased himself int a chair at the long dining table near a large window that overlooked the Tennessee River. Not being a big eater, he began to nibble some breakfast and sip hot coffee as he chatted quietly with his staff.

As Grant lifted his cup, the distant roar of rifle fire and dull rumble of artillery echoed through the dining room window, interrupting him. "Gentlemen," he said, setting down his coffee cup, "the ball is in motion!" As the staff mobilized, one of them helped Grant from his chair and handed him his crutch. Another staffer ran to Grant's command boat, the *Tigress*, to alert Captain Gwinn to get up steam for sailing and prepare for departure. To reach the boat from the back portico of the house, Grant had to cautiously descend the many steep steps of a three-tiered embankment to the Tennessee River below.

For Grant, it was all agonizingly slow. He was aware that, if the fighting had grown so intense that he could hear it eight miles away, it must be substantial. Aggravating his concern even more was the knowledge that he still had an hour-or-so trip upriver before he could reach the battlefield. As always with him, the uncertainty was worse than bad news.

As the *Tigress* steamed south, the boat passed Lew Wallace at Crump's Landing. Grant directed Captain Gwinn to swing in close and slow down. Grant hollered to Wallace to go to the fight by the nearest road—meaning the existing river road—and then the *Tigress* steamed on.

When Grant arrived at the fight, staffers lifted him onto his horse and stuck his crutch between his leg and the stirrup. His foot and leg were badly swollen and extremely painful, so he wore a house slipper on his left foot. He still had to have the foot in the stirrup, though, and in a downward position, which aggravated the injury and the pain level.

His discomfort was secondary to getting into the fight. His first commands were to order ammunition to every unit in the field. He remembered his quartermaster days in the old army and knew a

Maj. Gen. Lew Wallace would serve as one of the scapegoats of Shiloh and would spend decades trying to clear his name. In a footnote added to his memoir, written only months before his death, Grant finally absolved Wallace of any wrongdoing at the battle. By that point, Wallace had achieved worldwide fame for his mammoth best-selling novel, *Ben-Hur*. (loc)

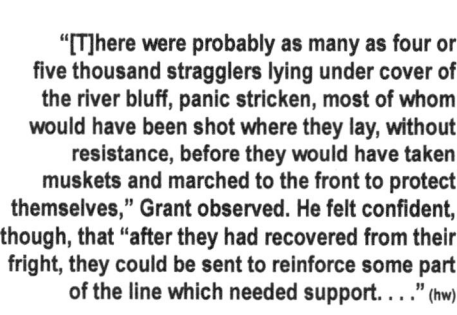

"[T]here were probably as many as four or five thousand stragglers lying under cover of the river bluff, panic stricken, most of whom would have been shot where they lay, without resistance, before they would have taken muskets and marched to the front to protect themselves," Grant observed. He felt confident, though, that "after they had recovered from their fright, they could be sent to reinforce some part of the line which needed support. . . ." (hw)

soldier with no ammunition was a soldier out of the fight—they always needed more ammunition.

He also addressed the chaos at the landing itself. Hundreds of Federal soldiers had broken before the Confederate onslaught and run back to the river, where they now cowered on the riverbank. Grant understood the shock they had experienced under fire, many of them for the first time; he also knew, if given time to collect themselves, many of them would return to the fight and be the good soldiers they could be. In the meantime, he ordered a pair of Iowa regiments to form a line and block any more men from running away from the battle. He impressed some cavalry into similar duty.

Events proved Grant right over time as the green troops gained experience. "Better troops never went upon a battle-field than many of these, officers and men, afterwards proved themselves to be, who fled panic-stricken at the first whistle of bullets and shell at Shiloh," Grant later wrote in exoneration.

Grant spent the day visiting every part of the field so he could see for himself what the situation was and

to let the men see him with them on the field, under fire with them. The men responded favorably to his presence, although the task itself proved harder than Grant expected. "The ground on which the battle was fought was undulating, heavily timbered with scattered clearings, the woods, giving some protection to the troops on both sides," Grant explained. "There was also considerable underbrush."

As he rode about, Grant personally visited every commander he could find. "I was continuously engaged in passing from one part of the field to another, giving directions to division commanders," he said. He spent only little time with Sherman, who held part of the Federal right. "His division was at that time wholly raw, no part of it ever having been in an engagement; but I thought this deficiency was more than made up by the superiority of the commander," Grant later said in his memoirs. "[H]is constant presence with them, inspired a confidence in officers and men that enabled them to render services on that bloody battle-field worthy of the best of veterans." Grant's assessment by the time of that writing may have been influenced by a 21-year friendship with Sherman, but the undeniable confidence Grant showed in his subordinate that day served as a formative, foundational block in that friendship.

With Confederates steadily pushing the Federals back toward the river, Grant sent an officer to find Lew Wallace and urge him to bring his 5,500 men to the battle as quickly as possible. Miscommunication and misunderstanding led to a delay, though, and Wallace would not arrive until near darkness, after fighting for the day had ceased, taking no part in the first day's fight and sparking a controversy about the march that has endured to this day.

Around 1:00 p.m., Don Carlos Buell arrived at Pittsburg Landing. He had actually arrived in Savannah the night before but had not notified Grant, who only found out after steaming up to the battlefield. Grant sent for him, but Buell seemed not to notice the urgency of the request and took his time to get there. When Buell finally arrived, he appeared mortified by the scene at the landing. Amidst the furor of hundreds of terrified men huddling on the riverbank, the frantic unloading of ammunition, and the wounded men being carried to the rear, Buell asked Grant when he was going to order a retreat across the river.

"Why, General Buell, I haven't despaired of whipping them yet!" Grant replied.

Buel began berating the stragglers and shaming them to rejoin their regiments. "He even threatened them with shells from the gunboats nearby," Grant noted.

*General, there's no need for all of that,* Grant said. *They're just scared. When they get control of themselves a bit, they'll go back into the fight. But right now, General, you could shoot them where they lie, and they're not going to get up and go back into the fight.* "Most of these men afterward proved themselves as gallant as any of those who saved the battle from which they had deserted," Grant later attested.

During the conference between the two generals, Capt. Irving Carson, one of Grant's scouts and a part-time correspondent for the *Chicago Tribune*, arrived with a report. Just then, a solid shot hit Carson in the face, taking his head off at the shoulders. The ball bounced on to take both legs off an officer walking up the bank from the Landing. Carson's blood and brains spattered Grant, who did his best to ignore, doubtless a show of resolve in front of his men from a man who was otherwise deeply uncomfortable with the sight of blood.

Grant ordered Buell to bring his army to the field. Buell spent the day bringing his army down the east side of the Tennessee River to a staging area so the navy could ferry them across. Buell would later claim that his Army of the Ohio had saved Grant from certain defeat that day—a claim Grant would flatly deny.

As Buell left to attend to his new duties, Grant turned his attention back to his commanders' progress, encouraging them to fight with a will as they grudgingly gave ground, falling back toward the river. He also directed his chief of ordinance, Col. J. B. Webster, to set up a strong artillery line along the road that led up from the landing—a line that became known as "Grant's Last Line of Defense." The road faced Dill Branch, some 20–25 feet deep with sharp banks, making it a formidable barrier for the Confederates on the other side. The artillery line provided protection for Grant's army as it fell back, giving the bedraggled men a place to rally.

Darkness fell and the fighting ceased as men in both armies collapsed in exhaustion on their arms. Rain began to fall on the battlefield. "During the night rain fell in torrents, and our troops were exposed to the storm without shelter," Grant recalled.

Grant, wearing his great coat, huddled under a tree to smoke a cigar, which proved hopeless in the rain. "My ankle was so much swollen from the fall of my horse that Friday night preceding, and the bruise was so painful, that I could get no rest," he added.

A monument marks the area in which Johnston was mortally wounded. "I do not question the personal courage of General Johnston, or his ability," Grant wrote of his Confederate counterpart. "But he did not win the distinction predicted for him by many of his friends. He did prove that as a general he was over-estimated." (cm)

**A monument in Shiloh National Cemetery marks the location of Grant's headquarters on the battlefield.** (cm)

"The drenching rain would have precluded the possibility of sleep without this additional cause."

"[G]rowing restive under the storm and the continuous pain," he finally retreated into the nearby Pitt Brothers Trading Post, where he had earlier made a headquarters. The surgeons had since made it into a field hospital. "The site was more unendurable than encountering the enemy's fire, and I returned to my tree in the rain," Grant confessed.

It was there, around midnight, that Sherman materialized out of the darkness and driving rain. He had come to urge Grant to retreat across the

Tennessee River, putting it between them and the Confederates. Grant stood, holding his lantern to push away the darkness between them.

"Well, Grant, we've had the Devil's own day today, haven't we," Sherman said, easing into the subject.

A long moment of rain passed as they faced each other in the lantern light. Grant took his cigar out of his mouth. "Yes," he replied. "Lick' em tomorrow, though."

Rain continued to pelt the leaves above them as Sherman considered the implications of Grant's statement: there would be no retreat. "Well, I guess I had better get back to my command," Sherman finally said.

"Best you do," Grant agreed. "And see to your men that they sleep on their arms. As I said at Fort Donelson, the army that attacks first will carry the day, and Confederates will have to get up mighty early in the morning to hit me before I hit him."

Sherman nodded, saluted, and disappeared back into the rain and darkness.

*   *   *

With the arrival of Wallace's division on the field and the arrival of Buell's army from across the river, Grant felt he had ample reinforcements to turn the tide of battle of April 7. "My command was thus nearly doubled in numbers and efficiency," he wrote.

As Grant predicted, fighting began at dawn, at first sporadic and tentative but soon developing into a full-roar cadence of ferocity terrible to hear.

The second day at Shiloh was essentially a reverse repeat of the first. Federals slowly pushed Confederates back across the same ground they had relinquished at such terrible cost the day before, with Confederates paying an equally terrible cost to lose it.

Around 1:00 p.m., as Grant and a pair of staff officers traveled the battlefield, they crossed through an open area that had looked safely deserted. But as soon as they got into the open, a fusillade of musketry and artillery fire erupted. The men put spurs to their horses as bullets and shells whistled around. Reaching the safety of the far wood line, they noticed one of the horses was panting heavily, shot clean through, right behind the rider's legs, just behind the saddle. "In a few minutes, the poor beast dropped dead; he had given no sign of injury until he came to a stop," Grant recalled.

Another of the men, Maj. John Hawkins, had lost his hat in the escape. He decided not to go back into the field to get it, then turned to Grant. "General, your sword," Hawkins pointed. The sword had taken a bullet just below the hilt, and sword and scabbard were both almost broken in half. In fact, by day's end, the sword would break entirely, and Grant would finish the battle of Shiloh with only a sword hilt. Grant's surgeon later pointed out that if he had not been wearing the sword, he would have taken a ball into the hip—a wound that certainly would have resulted in amputation. The survival rate for such wounds so close to the hip was low.

Grant put himself in peril one final time that day. Late in the afternoon, he rallied the remnants of Maj. Gen. Stephen Hurlburt's division against some rebels who needed a little "push" out of a woodlot. Grant organized the men into ranks and led them to where the firing was the heaviest, riding in front of them to prevent premature firing. When they reached effective range, he moved to their right to get out of the way, and yelled, "Charge!" It became the last charge Grant ever led. Although successful, it afterwards took on an inflated romance, perpetuated by enthusiastic journalists, that Grant led the final charge that carried the day at Shiloh.

By day's end, after Confederates withdrew from the field, Grant ordered Sherman to follow and probe: Were Confederates retreating or gathering for a counterattack? A final skirmish with Col. Nathan Bedford Forrest's cavalry at Fallen Timbers ended the action. Critics would claim Grant should have mounted a more robust pursuit, but Grant knew his men were exhausted. As Sherman attested, "We had just had two days of their 'Southern hospitality' and felt that if they were willing to leave us alone, we were happy to leave them alone."

Casualties from the two-day battle exceeded anything Americans north or south had ever conceived: 23,746 killed, wounded and missing. More Americans died at Shiloh than in all other American wars to that point combined. The Confederates suffered an especially grievous loss, Albert Sidney Johnston, mortally wounded on the first day.

Grant later remembered Shiloh as:

*the severest battle fought at the West during the war, and but few in the East equal that for hard, determined fighting. I saw an open field . . . so covered with dead that it would have been possible to walk across the clearing, in any direction, stepping on dead bodies without a foot touching on the ground.*

Although a Federal victory, the staggering human cost of the battle brought the country, North and South, to its knees and immediately sparked controversy and speculation. Lincoln faced heavy pressure to replace Grant, which he resisted.

"The battle of Shiloh . . . has been perhaps less understood, or, to state the case more accurately, more persistently misunderstood, than any other engagement . . . during the entire Rebellion," Grant contended.

Sherman agreed. "Probably no single battle of the war gave rise to such wild and damaging reports," he later observed. "It was publicly asserted at the North that our army was taken completely by surprise; that the rebels caught us in our tents; bayoneted the men in their beds; that General Grant was drunk; that Buell's opportune arrival saved the Army of the Tennessee from utter annihilation, etc." All proved untrue, although Buell and some of his subordinates agitated some of the trouble. Some of those accusations, particularly regarding Grant's drinking, remain today.

"We are all well and me as sober as a deacon," Grant assured Julia in the weeks after Shiloh. He urged her to ignore any gossip or criticism she might see in the papers. "I am very sorry to say a great deal of it originates in jealousy," he wrote. "This is far from applying, however, I think, to our Chief, Halleck, who I look upon as one of the greatest men of our age."

Publicly, though, Grant, "as usual, maintained an imperturbable silence," according to Sherman.

# $\mathcal{L}$*imbo*

## CHAPTER SIX
### *April–July 1862*

After the battle of Shiloh, Grant wrote Julia a letter in which he indicated how Shiloh had changed him and his outlook on the war. He admitted he had been one of those who felt the war would be a short and relatively bloodless one. Shiloh changed his mind. "I no longer feel this will be a short and bloodless war," he wrote. "I now feel it will be a long and bloody one; fought until one side or the other, holding principles so dear as unto death will have to yield those principles to the other side."

He did go on to say that, as bloody as Shiloh was, he was confident the Union would go on to ultimate victory. He gave three significant reasons for his convictions:

First, the South hit the Federals at Shiloh with the *best* leadership they had. The Confederate command at Shiloh reads like a "Who's Who" of military leadership at the time in America.

Second, the Confederates hit them with the *most* they had. As many as 45,000 Confederate soldiers swept across the battlefield—and this only seven weeks after the loss of a 13,000-man army at Fort Donelson. The ability to get together an army of that size in so short a time spoke much about the determination and

Grant's victory at Shiloh once more made him a victim of his own success—eager for action but sidelined by jealousy. (ac/cf)

zeal of the Confederacy to amass and move that many men across the Western theater so quickly.

Third, they hit them as *hard* as they could at Shiloh, and the Federals still prevailed. The courage and tenacity of the Confederate soldier at Shiloh was most impressive. He noted that "they hurled themselves against our positions again and again with no apparent concern for their own well-being, especially on the first day." However, the Federals still prevailed, and because of that, he felt the Union would ultimately prevail.

Newspapers held Grant responsible for the horrendous losses, but President Lincoln knew the casualty numbers were larger than anything anyone could comprehend because the numbers of men fighting in the battle were beyond anything anyone could comprehend. More than 100,000 men had fought at Shiloh over about 30 square miles of area. Lincoln knew those staggering numbers of combatants produced the equally staggering numbers of casualties. He would not relieve Grant from command.

"We are all well and me as sober as a deacon, no matter what is said to the contrary," Grant wrote to Julia. (ac/cm)

\* \* \*

Henry Halleck arrived at Pittsburg Landing on April 11. As historian Larry J. Daniel has pointed out, Halleck had never before commanded more than a platoon in the field, but he took over operational control of Grant's and Buell's combined armies, and then for good measure folded in a third army—John Pope's, recently victorious at Island No. 10. In total, Halleck' forces totaled some 120,000 men.

"Gen. Halleck is here, and I am truly glad of it," Grant told Julia in a letter.

That good feeling didn't last, though. As part of Halleck's reorganization, he named Grant as second-in-command of the department. On paper, it looked like a promotion, but in fact, it was a clever way for the ever-jealous Halleck to sideline Grant. The business of the army went around Grant rather than through him.

Grant chafed under the arrangement, but Halleck feigned innocence. "I am very much surprised, general, that you should find any cause of complaint in the recent assignment of commands. You

have precisely the position to which your rank entitles you . . ." Halleck wrote disingenuously a month later:

*You certainly will not suspect me of any intention to injure your feeling or reputation or to do you any injustice. For the last three months, I have done everything in my power to ward off the attacks which were made upon you. If you believe me your friend, you will not require explanation; if not, explanations on my part would be of little avail.*

Shortly after Halleck's arrival in the field, he directed his army group to begin the planned advance on Corinth. The movement was slow and ponderous, Halleck nervous about another surprise Confederate attack. As Grant described it, "The movement was a siege from the start to the close." Whenever the army stopped moving, Halleck ordered the men to immediately dig in. It took the army the better part of a month to advance 20 miles—a distance that should have taken only a couple of days.

In one of the most effective tricks of the war, Confederate commander P. G. T. Beauregard—Johnston's replacement—evacuated Corinth at the last minute, right under Halleck's nose. By the time the Federal commander ordered an attack, the

**According to the National Park Service, "From Late April into May 1862, the region around Corinth witnessed the largest concentration of military forces on United States soil up to that time. Three Union armies totaled 111,400 men. Two Confederate armies reported 112,000 men on the books, but of these, only 70,500 were present in early May."** (ac/cm)

Artist Adolph Metzner sketched the army near the Mississippi state line as it marched toward Corinth. (loc)

Willam T. Sherman was friends with both Grant and Halleck, and he tried to strike a middle course between them. As they shared time in the field, though, Grant and Sherman grew increasingly close and increasingly loyal to each other. Alluding to gossip that plagued each of them, Sherman said, "Grant stood by me when I was crazy, and I stood by him when he was drunk, and now we stand by each other always." (loc)

army found Quaker guns—logs painted to look like cannons—and a town empty of any enemy soldiers.

In the following weeks of mostly inactivity, Grant wrote to Julia about his enforced idleness and said that he could be at the farthest reach of the territory under his command and be of the same usefulness. "My position was so embarrassing in fact that I made several applications during the siege to be relieved," Grant later said. His requests went unheeded, and he finally decided to resign.

Sherman caught wind of Grant's decision and came to see him. He found his friend packing his trunk.

*Don't do it,* Sherman told him. *You will regret it the moment you get home.* Sherman urged patience, convinced "some happy accident might restore him [Grant] to favor and his true place."

Instead, Sherman suggested that Grant ask Halleck if he could re-locate his headquarters—to Memphis, perhaps—which would get Grant out from under Halleck's thumb. Halleck, eager to be rid of Grant, readily agreed. By June 22, Grant was northward bound.

Along the way, Confederates nearly captured him. As Grant and his small group of staff officers arrived in Collierville, some 20 miles outside of Memphis, a local doctor tipped off Confederate cavalry about Grant's presence after Grant stopped at a local home for a glass of water. Grant, oblivious to the danger, rode away just before the cavalry arrived to scoop him up. Assuming Grant had too much of a head start, the cavalry didn't pursue, missing the chance to overtake him just a couple miles down the road, asleep on the ground in the shade of some trees, waiting for the sun to go down before continuing into Memphis in the cool of the evening.

*   *   *

On July 11, the "happy accident" Sherman predicated came to pass. Halleck received a telegram from the War Department telling him of his appointment to General in Chief of the Army, with headquarters in Washington City. Halleck's reputation as "Old Brains" and the string of victories he had apparently engineered in the Western Theater—in fact, Grant's victories that Halleck had taken credit for—had earned Lincoln's favor.

That same day, Halleck wired to Grant and called him to Corinth.

Grant arrived on July 15, still in the dark as to why it was going to be his headquarters. Halleck remained uncommunicative and, by the time he left Mississippi on July 17, he had still not told Grant about the promotion to general in chief and the call to Washington.

Not until October 25 would Grant receive an official appointment to the position of department commander, although for all intents he acted in that capacity following Halleck's departure. No one in the department outranked him, and he reported directly to the general in chief.

But he had considerable territory to oversee, filled with hostile residents. His forces were so scattered as to be ineffectual. And his superior offered no clear strategic plan to follow.

A member of the West Point Class of 1829, Joseph E. Johnston rose higher in the U.S. Army than his classmate, Robert E. Lee. "Take it all in all, the South, in my opinion, had no better soldier than Joe Johnston," Grant would later say. "I have had nearly all of the Southern generals in high command in front of me, and Joe Johnston gave me more anxiety than any of the others. I was never half so anxious about Lee." Johnston's wounding outside Richmond in late May 1862 would put him on a course to eventually confront Grant in the west. (loc)

# Northern Mississippi

## CHAPTER SEVEN

### *July–December 1862*

Despite his move east, Halleck seemed unable to let go of his former plans in Grant's department. "I have studied out and can finish the campaign in the West," Halleck wrote to Sherman. As a result, he placed Grant in command of the department but didn't empower him to take action. However, the immense amount of work Halleck faced in his new job—not to mention the geographical immediacy of events in the East—consumed the new general-in-chief and prevented him from ever executing whatever plans for the West he'd once concocted—if any.

For Grant, the next few months constituted another period of limbo, different from those he'd faced after Donelson or Shiloh. The great 130,000-man army that had marched into an evacuated and empty Corinth back on May 30 now stretched scattered over several hundred square miles of territory with a hostile population. For the next few months, Halleck's dithering pinned him in place trying to maintain control of a district that encompassed West Tennessee from Memphis up to Columbus, Kentucky on the Mississippi river to Jackson, Tennessee, and down to Grand Junction, Tennessee.

With his forces spread over southwest Tennessee and northern Mississippi, Grant found himself in the fall of 1862 covering a large swath of territory with no clear objective. He would eventually take matters into his own hands. (ac/cf)

In Memphis, Grant established headquarters at the Hunt home not far from the Mississippi River. His staff set up a tent for him in the front yard, where he slept at night; by day, he worked in the roomy mansion. To protect the house's beautiful wood floors, he ordered staff and soldiers to take off their shoes or boots when entering. (loc)

Grant felt vulnerable and on the defensive—a position to which he was not accustomed. "The most anxious period of the war, to me, was during the time the Army of the Tennessee was guarding the territory acquired by the fall of Corinth and Memphis, and before I was sufficiently reinforced to take the offensive," he later admitted.

Compounding his woes, he kept facing calls to send men to reinforce Buell's Army of the Ohio, which the War Department had sent to Chattanooga. By early September, Grant was down to around 50,000 men.

Meanwhile, lurking just to the south, Confederate forces under Maj. Gen. Earl Van Dorn—recently reassigned from duty in Vicksburg, Mississippi—and Maj. Gen. Sterling Price—freshly arrived from Missouri—posed a problem. Their untethered forces could move fast, potentially striking at Grant's divided forces before they could consolidate. Grant received orders to prevent Van Dorn and Price from joining with the Confederate forces that had escaped from Corinth, now commanded by Gen. Braxton Bragg.

In mid-September, Grant ordered a coordinated assault by two of his division commanders, Brig. Gen. Edward O. C. Ord and Brig. Gen. William S. Rosecrans, against Price's troops, isolated in Iuka, Mississippi. Poor roads delayed Rosecrans's march, and Grant worried that he might not arrive in time, so he changed the plan and ordered Ord not to attack until Rosecrans arrived and engaged first. Ignorant of the change, Rosecrans arrived on the afternoon of September 19 and attacked—but an acoustic shadow, a trick of the terrain that blocked sound, prevented

Ord from hearing anything. Rosecrans eventually drove off the Confederates but didn't score a decisive victory that would have let him effectively pursue. The Confederates escaped and soon joined forces with Van Dorn.

"I was disappointed at the result of the battle of Iuka," Grant admitted, "but I had so high an opinion of General Rosecrans that I found no fault at the time."

Rosecrans, for his part, was furious about the lack of support and the lost opportunity, and the episode bloomed into "the beginning of a misunderstanding which grew into positive dislike between Grant and Rosecrans—a breach that never healed," according to brigade commander Col. John Fuller, one of Rosecrans's subordinates.

Grant's initial report of the battle praised Rosecrans, but as the controversy grew between them—and as outside critics pointed fingers at both generals and the missed opportunity—Grant's story evolved, growing ever more critical of Rosecrans, who grew ever more aggrieved. "You have had no truer friend nor more loyal sub ordinate under your command than myself . . ." Rosecrans complained to Grant.

Even a follow-up battle at Corinth October 3–4 did little to diffuse tensions. Van Dorn tried to retake the rail junction by launching a surprise attack with

Grant spent most of the fall of 1862 protecting the railroads from guerillas. The Confederate attempt to retake the rail junction at Corinth in October proved a much more serious—albeit more tangible—threat. (ac/cm)

A copy of Keith Rocco's *The Battle of Corinth* hangs in the Corinth Battlefield visitor center. (cm)

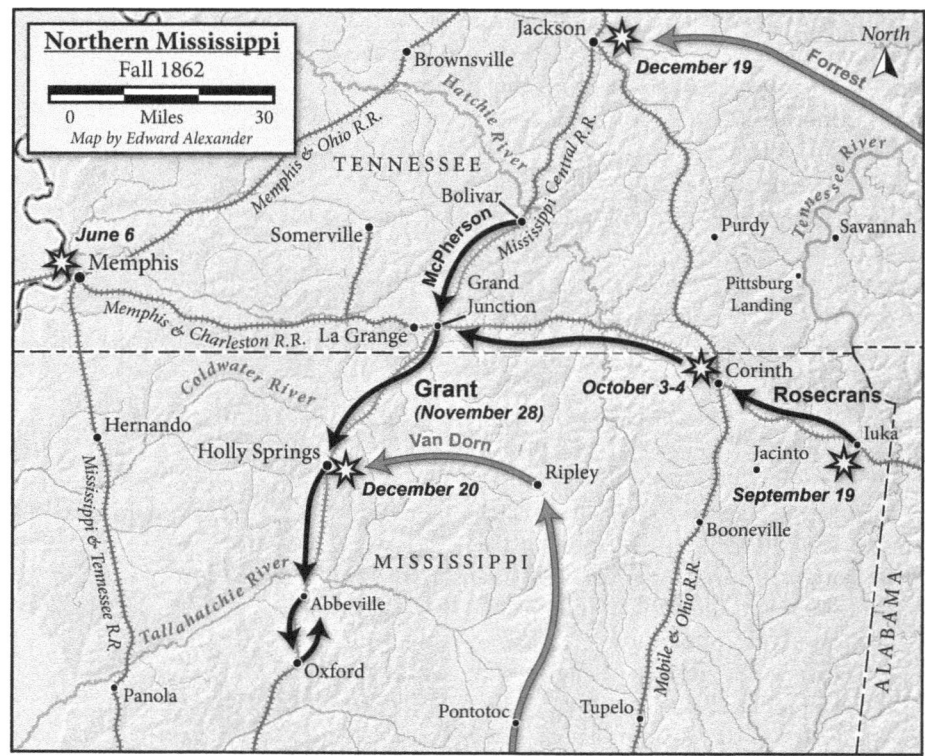

NORTHERN MISSISSIPPI, FALL
1862—The fall of Memphis
opened the Mississippi
River for Federal moves
farther south, but Halleck's
inattention to operations in
the theater left Grant stuck
in southern Tennessee and
northeast Mississippi for
months, mostly defending
the Memphis & Charleston
Railroad. On November 2,
he ordered a consolidation
of forces at La Grange and,
on November 28, began
a southward thrust into
Mississippi with an eye on
fighting his way toward
Vicksburg from the north.

about 22,000 men. Rosecrans, overseeing the town's
defenses, had about 23,000 men. On the first day of the
battle, Confederates met with initial success, piercing
the Federal line, but waning daylight prevented Van
Dorn from further exploiting his advantage. It likewise
prevented Rosecrans from executing a counterattack.
The battle culminated the next day with a series of
uncoordinated Confederate attacks, but Rosecrans's
stout defense held.

The Federal victory did little to diffuse tensions
between the former friends. Grant tried to exert
his authority over Rosecrans, and Rosecrans began
to balk. "I am forced to say," Rosecrans demanded
indignantly, "that if you do not meet me frankly with
a declaration that you are satisfied I shall consider my
power to be useful in this department ended." While
he did not threaten to resign, Rosecrans did say in
private correspondence to Halleck that he intended to
passive-aggressively resist Grant's authority.

On October 23, Halleck ordered Grant to send
Rosecrans to Cincinnati. The assignment came with a
promotion to major general and command of the Army

of the Ohio, replacing Don Carlos Buell, who had fallen out of favor with Washington. "I was delighted at the promotion of General Rosecrans to a separate command . . ." Grant later wrote. "As a subordinate I found that I could not make him do as I wished, and had determined to relieve him from duty that very day."

Grant's account has the flavor of a judgment written 20 years after the fact and colored by subsequent events. Neither man knew in October what Grant knew writing his memoirs years later; the curdled friendship between the two men would get even more sour.

*   *   *

Grant later characterized these months after Halleck's departure as a time of "much fighting between small bodies of the contending armies, but these encounters were dwarfed by the magnitude of the main battles so as to be now almost forgotten except by those engaged in them." For Grant, it felt like death by a million paper cuts.

On October 25, he received formal appointment as department commander. By the first week of November, he developed plans to take the initiative against the next strategic target: Vicksburg, Mississippi. Located on a high bluff over the Mississippi River midway between Memphis and New Orleans, Vicksburg gave Confederates control over a key stretch of the river, preventing Federal control of north-south traffic while keeping open a vital east-west route of supplies for the South. The city was the nail head that kept the two halves of the Confederacy together, said Jefferson Davis. Abraham Lincoln likewise recognized the city as "the key."

Grant sent a telegram to Halleck outlining plans for a move on the "Key City." He intended to use the Mississippi Central Railroad as his supply line south to the Mississippi capital of Jackson, then wheel to the west and march the 50 or so miles to Vicksburg and take the city from the land side. In preparation, Grant began storing supplies at Holly Springs, Mississippi, a few miles below Memphis on the Mississippi Central line.

"I approve of your plan of advancing upon the enemy as soon as you are strong enough for that

**Fewer relationships in Grant's career remain as puzzling as his relationship with Maj. Gen. William S. Rosecrans. Over time, Grant changed his story about Rosecrans's performance at the battle of Iuka, beginning with praise but later brimming with criticism. Scant documentation exists to shed light on why their relationship deteriorated.** (loc)

purpose," Halleck replied. "I hope for an active campaign on the Miss. this fall." By that point, Grant had already mobilized his force in preparation for the move.

During this time, Grant had his first real experience with the practicalities of the recently announced Emancipation Proclamation. The final proclamation was not due to go into effect until January 1, 1863, but already, enslaved people flocked to Grant's army seeking protection. "Orders of the government prohibited the expulsion of the negroes from the protection of the army, when they came in voluntarily," Grant wrote. "Humanity forbade allowing them to starve."

The sheer numbers presented a massive logistical issue for Grant, who solved the problem by employing the former slaves on the region's many deserted plantations. Corn and cotton were ripe, so the government paid them to pick and gin the cotton, which the quartermaster's department shipped northward for sale. From those proceeds, "a fund was created not only sufficient to feed and clothe all . . . but to build them comfortable cabins, hospitals for the sick, and to supply them with many comforts they have never known before," declared Grant. "At once the freedmen became self-sustaining." Grant ever after believed the endeavor served as "the first idea of a 'Freedman's Bureau.'"

During this time, Grant first met a man who would play a major role in his later successes: Flag-Officer David Dixon Porter of the U.S. Navy. Porter had been sent to Memphis to coordinate a joint army-navy operation down the Mississippi with Maj. Gen. John McClernand, who was on leave from Grant's army and attempting to raise a group of soldiers he could command independently. Porter and Grant hit it off immediately, and as Porter told him, "I am ready to cooperate with anybody and everybody." Grant would soon take Porter up on that offer.

Word of McClernand's effort circulated quickly. "McClernand is announced as forming a grand army to Sweep the Mississippi when the truth is he is in Springfield Illinois trying to be elected to the U.S. Senate," William T. Sherman told his younger brother, John Sherman, himself a U.S. Senator from Ohio. Sherman disliked McClernand, a sentiment that would only worsen as the two men spent more time together.

Grant, meanwhile, tried to get to the bottom of the machinations. Lincoln and Secretary of War Edwin Stanton may have been trying to hedge their bets with the McClernand initiative, but for once, Halleck—whose dislike for McClernand outweighed his jealously of Grant—gave Grant the trump card he needed. "You have command of all troops sent to your department, and have permission to fight the enemy where you please," the General in Chief told Grant. Halleck even lent a hand by slow-walking McClernand's arrangements.

On December 5, as Grant and Sherman converged on Oxford, Mississippi, Halleck sent Grant a strong hint that someone should be in Memphis to gather up McClernand's newly arriving recruits before McClernand himself got there on December 20. "[T]he largest number possible" should be thrown upon Vicksburg with the Gunboats," Halleck suggested. Grant sent Sherman to assume command of the troops and head downriver with Porter. Grant, meanwhile, continued his push southward along the rail line, still aiming for Vicksburg by land.

**The issuance of the Emancipation Proclamation in mid-September turned Grant's army into a magnet for self-emancipating slaves. Grant was one of the first Union officers to establish a self-sustaining solution for what otherwise would have been a serious logistical problem.** (ac/cm)

A friend of Jefferson Davis's, Maj. Gen. Earl Van Dorn (left) boasted a fine reputation but little to show for it. Retaking Corinth had offered a chance at redemption; that failure led to his reassignment to the cavalry, where he finally shone. (loc)

Confederate cavalryman Nathan Bedford Forrest (right) summed up his philosophy of war in a single pithy line: "Get 'em skeered, then keep the skeer on 'em." (loc)

No sooner had Sherman mobilized the expedition than dual disasters struck Grant. On December 19, Confederate cavalryman Nathan Bedford Forrest struck one of Grant's rearward supply bases in Jackson, Tennessee. Then, on December 20, another Confederate cavalry raid under Earl Van Dorn struck Grant's supply base at Holly Springs.

With all of Grant's supplies in ashes at the Holly Springs train depot, locals laughed at the Yankee misfortune. *What's your army going to eat now?* they sneered.

*The same thing you are,* Grant replied—and then he sent out foraging parties 15 miles to either side of the line of march to secure food as the army slowly moved north back to Grand Junction. Southern sneers turned to impotent anger as Grant's men lived off the land—a lesson that would serve him well in the months to come.

\*    \*    \*

Aside from the damage done by the cavalry raids, Grant suffered a self-inflicted wound in that same period. On December 17, Grant issued General Order 11, which stated, "The Jews, as a class, violating every regulation of trade established by the Treasury Department, and also Department orders, are hereby expelled from the Department."

Word of the order didn't reach Washington until January 4. Lincoln, stunned, immediately "deemed it necessary to revoke it." Halleck ordered Grant to rescind it, which he dutifully did on January 7.

The controversial order may have sprung from an unlikely source. Grant's father, Jesse—always quick to try and capitalize on Grant's success, much to Grant's annoyance—appeared in camp in mid-December, bringing in tow three cotton speculators, Jewish brothers named Mack. They hoped Jesse could prevail upon his son to issue them cotton-trading permits. Initially, Grant was furious that they had "entrapped his old father into such an unworthy undertaking." His anger quickly turned to embarrassment, though, when he discovered the Mack brothers had offered Jesse twenty-five percent of the profits. General Order 11 was a gross overreaction to the situation.

The order remained a blot remained a blot on Grant for the rest of his life. During his 1868 run for the presidency, Order 11 not surprisingly became a campaign issue. "I do not pretend to sustain the order," Grant told a Jewish supporter:

Jesse Grant bragged about his oldest son, "my Ulysses," and he vociferously defended him publicly and in the press. However, he also tried on several occasions to profit from his son's position, which always angered Grant. (loc)

> *The order was made and sent out, without any reflection, and without thinking of the Jews as a sect or race to themselves, but simply as the persons who had successfully . . . violated an order. . . . I have no prejudice against sect or race but want each individual to be judged by his own merit. Order No. 11 does not sustain this statement, I admit, but then I do not sustain that order.*

Grant might have suffered more immediate fallout from General Order 11 but that it came on the heels of a wave of grim news: the Army of the Potomac had been beaten at Fredericksburg on December 13; Rosecrans's newly christened Army of the Cumberland had been brutalized December 31–January 2; and closest to home for Grant, Sherman's expeditionary force had been bloodily repulsed outside Vicksburg at Chickasaw Bayou. All of these military setbacks provided the context for the final Emancipation Proclamation, which needed military victories to give it teeth.

And as one last poke in the eye for Grant, McClernand had shown up in Memphis and then steamed south to take command of the troops Sherman had commandeered from him.

Grant decided it was time to take the field again himself.

*Vicksburg*

## CHAPTER EIGHT
*January–July 1863*

Grant and his army spent the first four months of 1863 trying in vain to get at Vicksburg. They tried constructing two different canals to bypass the "Confederate Gibraltar." They blew up levees and flooded terrain. With Porter's full support, they tried naval expeditions through twisting bayous.

The Mississippi River system worked against them the entire time. "The Mississippi is, perhaps, the most tortuous stream in the world," wrote Grant aide Adam Badeau. "Its course is frequently north, east, south, and west, within a circuit of twenty miles." The shifting course of the river continually created an "intricate network of bayous."

The weather, too, worked against them. "The long, dreary, and, for heavy and continuous rains and high water, unprecedented winter was one of great hardship to all engaged about Vicksburg," Grant admitted. As a result, wrote Badeau, "The camps were frequently submerged, and the diseases consequent to this exposure prevailed among the troops ; dysenteries and fevers made sad havoc, and the small-pox even was introduced. . . ."

Years later, Grant tried to put a happy face on this period of struggle. "All these failures would have

The tree beneath which Grant and Pemberton met was soon reduced to splinters by soldiers anxious for a souvenir to remember the meeting. Here, Curt Fields sits with Morgan Gates, a licensed battlefield guide at Vicksburg who portrays John Pemberton, beneath a similar tree during the Civil War Sesquicentennial. (bs)

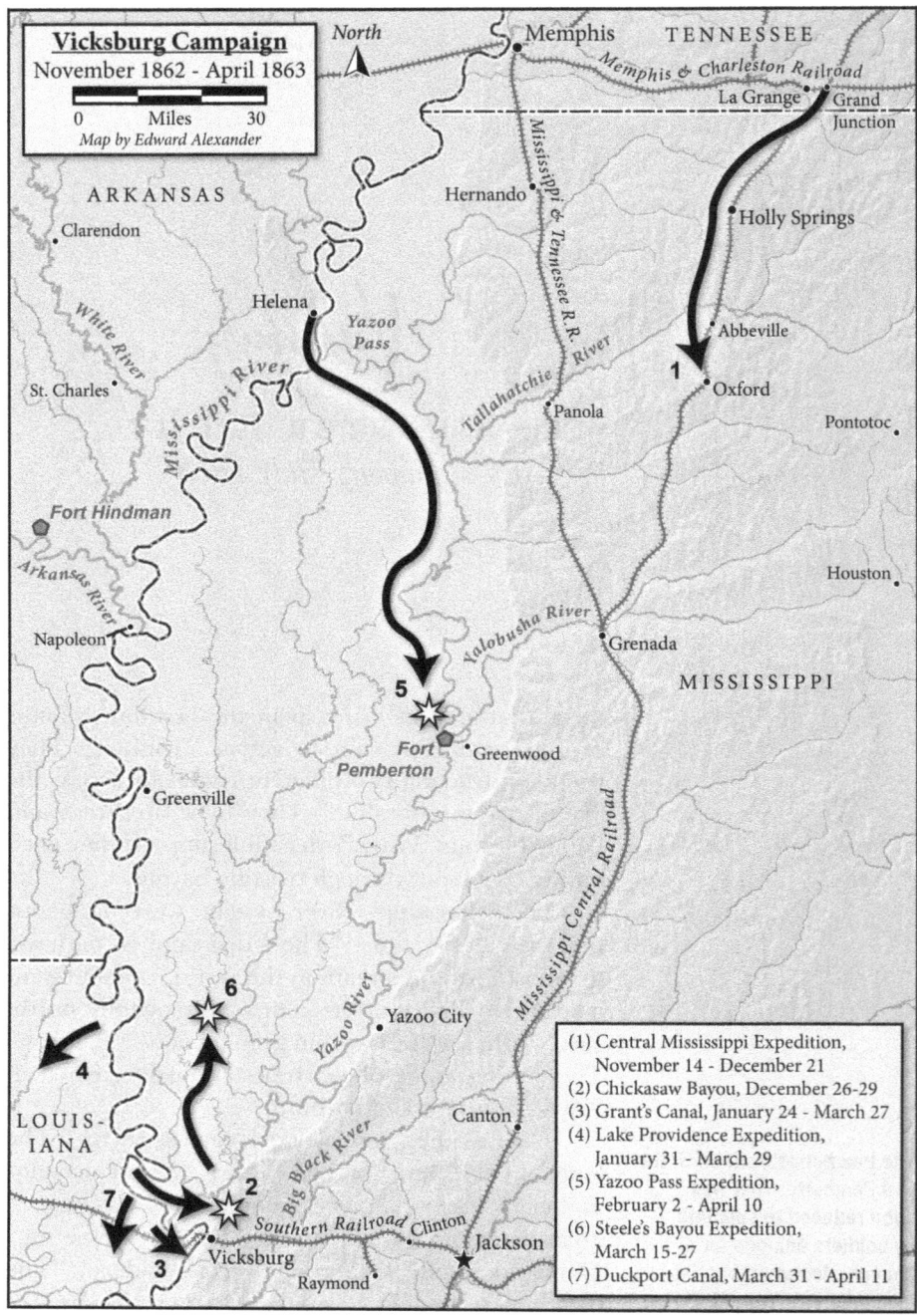

VICKSBURG CAMPAIGN, NOVEMBER 1862–APRIL 1863—After the aborted overland attempt at Vicksburg in December 1862 (1), Grant spent the early months of 1863 looking for other ways to get at or around Vicksburg. He tried direct assaults, maneuvers, feats of engineering, and joint operations with the U.S. Navy. Weather, water, and disease worked against him—as did Confederates. Political pressure mounted as the months ticked away, but Grant remained patient.

Vicksburg—also known as the Hill City—was the second-largest settlement in the state. On the eve of the Civil War, some 5,000 people lived there, including 3,500 white residents and another 1,500 black residents, the majority of whom were enslaved. Its position on the Mississippi River, midway between Memphis and New Orleans, made it the busiest port in the state. (loc)

been very discouraging if I had expected much from the efforts; but I had not," he wrote in his memoirs. At the time, though, he expressed his frustration to Julia: "I am very well but much perplexed. Hitherto, I have had nothing to do but fight the enemy. This time I have to overcome obstacles to reach him."

Had any of the attempts panned out, Grant was ready to exploit them, but the main result of the work was to occupy his men, who otherwise had nothing to do unless Grant kept them busy. The efforts also worked to quell public discontent about the war effort in the west, although people, politicians, and the press grew more restive as winter gave way to spring. Whispering against Grant grew intense as the setbacks piled up. Halleck even claimed, "the President . . . seems to be rather impatient about matters on the Mississippi," although no written proof of that has surfaced.

Stories do survive of Lincoln coming to Grant's defense, though. "No man will ever know how much trouble I have had to carry my point about him," the president lamented. "The opposition from several of our best Republicans has been so bitter that I could hardly resist it." Perhaps chief among those Republicans was the disgruntled McClernand, who went so far as to try and advance rumors that Grant

GRANT'S CANAL

During the summer of 1862, the Federals' first attempt to bypass Vicksburg by digging a canal across DeSoto Peninsula failed.
By January, 1863, the Federals had reoccupied the Louisiana shore
opposite Vicksburg. Gen. U. S. Grant ordered work on the canal
resumed. The canal was to be 60 feet wide, one and one-half
miles long, and deep enough to float any vessel on the river.
Ground was broken on January 30. Negro work gangs assisted
by fatigue details from the Union Army began the work. Later,
steam pumps and dredge boats were employed. To stop the work,
the Confederates emplaced several big guns on the shore opposite
the canal's exit but the work progressed. On March 7, the upper
dam gave way, flooding the entire peninsula. "Grant's Canal"
had failed.

**A small unit of Vicksburg National Military Park sits on the Louisiana bank of the Mississippi that preserves a final vestige of Grant's canal.** (cm)

was drinking again. Lincoln tried to brush them aside, as illustrated by a famous but untrue story. "Do you know where Grant buys his whiskey?" the president supposedly asked a group of Grant's critics. "I would like to present some to other generals not so successful." ("That would have been very good if I had said it," Lincoln once admitted.)

While the story has become apocryphal, McClernand's jealousy was anything but. Grant's presence in the field irked him because McClernand otherwise would have been senior man. "I have been deprived of the command that has been committed to me," he complained to Secretary of War Stanton. After Grant's arrival in January, McClernand tried to exert independent authority by throwing around his political weight: "I am invested, by order of the Secretary of War, indorsed by the President, and by order of the President communicated to you by the General-in-Chief, with the command of all the forces operating on the Mississippi River. . . ."

Grant—with Halleck's backing—poo-pooed him. McClernand backed down, but tensions remained. "McClernand was still intriguing against General Grant, in hopes to regain the command of the whole expedition," Sherman noted, "and . . . others were raising a clamor against General Grant in the newspapers at the North."

It would prove to be one of Grant's most challenging periods of the war.

*   *   *

In all events, Grant knew time was against him now that spring had arrived. On April 16, he decided to break the stalemate by sending troops and supplies past the city by water. That would require running the vaunted river batteries. "Porter, as was always the case with him, not only acquiesced in the plan, but volunteered to use his entire fleet as transports. I had intended to make this request, but he anticipated me," Grant wrote, noting the close working relationship and strong faith in each other the two men had developed. Porter's only warning was that once the ships passed downriver of the city, "we give up all hopes of ever getting them up again" because of the strength of the Mississippi's current, which would expose the gunboats to extended fire if they tried to chug back upriver.

The successful move stunned the Confederates. "I regard navigation of the Mississippi River as shut out from us now," Pemberton wrote to Jefferson Davis. "No more supplies can be gotten from the Trans-Mississippi Department."

However, the move downriver was just the first phase in Grant's plan. For the next step, he asked

**"The sight was magnificent, but terrible," Grant said after watching Porter's guns run past the Vicksburg batteries.** (loc)

**Grant's partnership with Adm. David Dixon Porter became one of the most important ingredients to his overall success.** (loc)

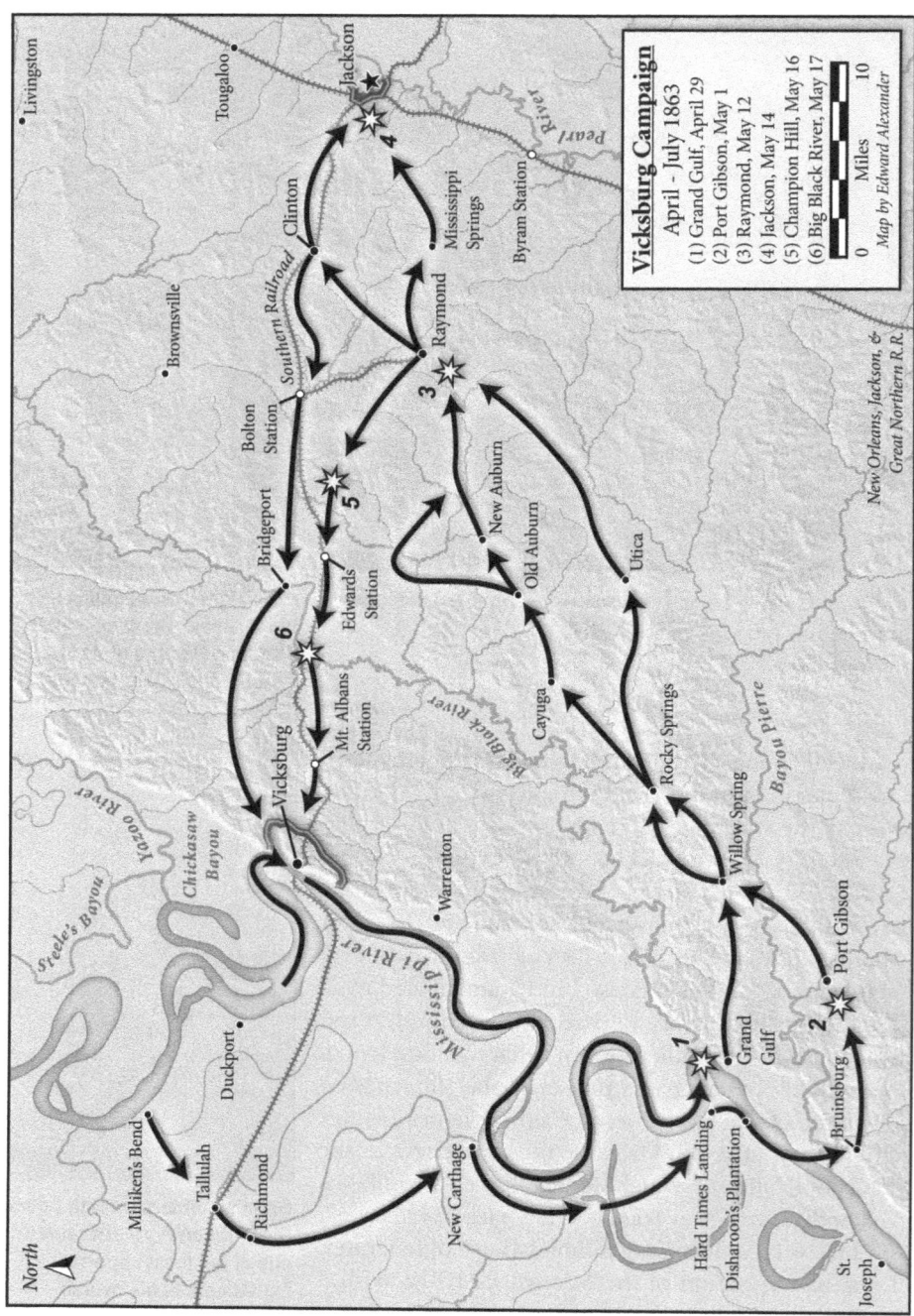

**VICKSBURG CAMPAIGN, APRIL–JULY 1863**—After crossing the Mississippi River, Grant's army fought five battles in seventeen days. Grant established a beachhead at Port Gibson, secured a supply route through Grand Gulf, then struck into the state's interior. After severing the Confederate railroad, Grant's army then moved in on Vicksburg from the landward side.

the navy to ferry his army from the west bank of the Mississippi to the east. On April 30–May 1, without losing a man or animal, Porter's boats transported two-thirds of Grant's army across the river without any Confederate resistance.

Grant understood the tremendous stakes of the moment—the risk he faced as well as the possible reward. "I was now in the enemy's country, with a vast river and the stronghold of Vicksburg between me and my base of supplies," Grant later observed.

For Federal forces, the first four months of 1863 consisted of a lot of time marching through swamps, bogs, and bayous. (hw)

"But I was on dry ground on the same side of the river with the enemy."

Sherman, for one, was deeply skeptical of the entire operation. "[I]t is not a good plan," he wrote to his politician brother. "We commit a great mistake." To his credit, though, he presented his objections directly to Grant, verbally and in writing. Such was their relationship, they spoke freely, even as commander and subordinate. "We often met casually, regardless of rank or power, and talked and gossiped of things in general, as officers do and should," Sherman later recalled when writing of the conversation.

Sherman argued in favor of abandoning operations along the river and, instead, returning to the overland route through Holly Springs and Oxford. Grant listened patiently and filed the objections away before carrying ahead with his plan to move south.

"General Grant would not, for reasons other than military, take any course which looked like a step backward," Sherman wrote in hindsight. Indeed, as Grant himself admitted in his own memoirs years later, "One of my superstitions had always been when I started to go any where, or to do anything, not to turn back, or stop until the thing intended was accomplished." The Vicksburg campaign would not be the last time Grant's "superstition" would guide his decision making.

In the end, Sherman promised Grant, "Whatever plan of action [you] may adopt it will receive from me the same zealous co-operation and energetic support as though conceived by myself."

As Grant later recounted it, "I did not regard . . . the conversation between us or the letter . . . as protests, but simply friendly advice which the relations between us fully justified. Sherman gave the same energy to make the campaign a success that he would or could have done if it had been ordered by himself."

By the evening of May 18—after Grant had successfully plunged into the interior of Jefferson Davis's home state, won five battles in 17 days, and closed on Vicksburg from the landward side—Sherman was willing to eat crow. He and Grant found themselves overlooking the scene of Sherman's failed December assaults at Chickasaw Bayou. *I felt no positive assurance of success for this campaign*, Sherman admitted. *But here we are, at the end of one of the greatest campaigns in history. You ought to make a report of it at once.*

*Vicksburg is not yet captured*, Grant replied. *There is no telling what might happen before it's taken.*

*Captured or not*, Sherman said, *this was a complete and successful campaign.*

*       *       *

"Here we have begun a move that is one of the most dangerous in War," Sherman had told his wife at the start of the maneuver.

Once across the river, Grant fought a battle at Port Gibson on May 1, which also allowed him to outflank a Confederate bastion at Grand Gulf. The navy had failed to take Grand Gulf a few days earlier, but Grant now met them there and, while there, made one of the most consequential decisions of the war.

First, though, Grant took a bath. "I had not been with my baggage since the 27th of April and consequently had had no change of underclothing, no meal except such as I could pick up sometimes at other headquarters, and no tent to cover me," he explained. He borrowed fresh underclothing from one of the navy officers, then ate a hot meal and caught up on his mail.

One letter came from Maj. Gen. Nathaniel Banks, who was then supposed to be trying to capture the Confederate stronghold of Port Hudson, Louisiana, 120 miles to the south as the crow flew but much farther as the steamboat chugged. Banks's letter notified Grant of a delay in his expedition to the interior.

This changed Grant's plans immediately. Halleck had wanted "your forces and those of General Banks [to] be brought into co-operation as early as possible." Grant had led Halleck to believe he would make this juncture, but Grant didn't really want to carry out the move because Banks outranked him. After months of trying to crack Vicksburg's shell, Grant didn't want Banks to get the credit for any success that would come after joining forces with Grant. By the time Grant had crossed the river, he had resolved to detach only McClernand's XIII Corps—which would serve double duty by getting rid of the problematic McClernand—but if Banks wasn't even in place, McClernand's detachment would only be wasted, while the Confederates would use the extra time to improve their fortifications.

"I therefore determined to move independently of Banks, cut loose from my base, destroy the rebel force in rear of Vicksburg and invest or capture the city," Grant decided. He knew "Halleck's caution would lead him to disapprove of this course," so rather than ask for permission, he would ask for forgiveness. "The time it would take to communicate with Washington and get a reply would be so great that I could not be interfered with until it was demonstrated whether my plan was practicable," he reasoned.

The choice changed the course of the war for, had Grant gone to meet Banks, the story of Vicksburg's fall would have played out differently and the trajectory of Grant's career changed entirely.

Grant ever after liked to perpetuate the story that he "cut loose from his base." He mentions it several times in his memoirs, and it has become part of the Vicksburg myth. In fact, as a former quartermaster, he knew the value of a secure supply line. While his men did, in part, live off the land as they moved into Mississippi's interior, Grant also made sure there was a secure supply line, overseen by Maj. Gen. Francis Blair's division of Sherman's corps.

On May 12, Grant's forces fought a battle at Raymond. From there, Grant intended to fall on the Southern Railroad, but instead he made an impromptu decision to move toward the state capital

The Bowman House Hotel, the finest in Jackson, hosted Confederate General Joseph E. Johnston one night and, in the very same room, Federal General Ulysses S. Grant the next. (cm)

of Jackson. Word had reached Grant of a Confederate force gathering there under Gen. Joseph E. Johnston. "Even then the ability of General Johnston was recognized," Sherman said, "and General Grant told me that he was about the only general on that side whom he feared."

On May 14, Grant's army drove Johnston's small force out of Jackson, and on May 16, Grant then turned on John Pemberton at a country crossroads east of Vicksburg called Champion Hill. On May 17, Grant then overran Pemberton's rear guard at the Big Black River bridge, driving Pemberton back into the city and bottling him up. This is the move that also gave Grant access to the waterways of Chickasaw Bayou, which allowed a renewed connection with the navy. Grant immediately ordered the establishment of a new supply line.

"Hard tack! Hard tack!" the men would cry as Grant rode the lines.

*We have been engaged ever since our arrival in building a road over which to supply you with everything you need,* Grant told them, urging just a little more patience.

The cry, he said, "instantly changed to cheers."

Grant's army arrived on the outskirts of Vicksburg

**The 15-foot-high bronze statue of Grant at Vicksburg was sculpted by Frederick C. Hibbard and dedicated in 1918 at a cost of $34,000. It depicts Grant seated atop one of his favorite horses, Kangaroo. (cm)**

on May 18, hot on Confederate heels. Riding the momentum he'd built over the previous two weeks, Grant assaulted Vicksburg the next day, on May 19. "Johnston was in my rear, only fifty miles away . . ." he reasoned. "There was danger of his coming to the assistance of Pemberton." However, the attacks were scattered and piecemeal, and they failed. So, he tried a more concentrated, coordinated set of assaults on May 22, but they, too, failed. That afternoon, Grant ordered the commencement of siege operations.

"After the recent string of Federal victories, the troops believed they could carry the works on their front," Grant later explained, "and would not have worked so patiently in the trenches if they had not been allowed to try."

\*    \*    \*

The siege of Vicksburg lasted 47 days. "[T]he enemy was limited in supplies of food, men, and munitions of war to what they had on hand," Grant knew. He only needed "to 'out-camp the enemy,' as it were, and to incur no more losses."

During that time, Grant reinforced his army, oversaw construction of fortifications, and kept a wary eye out for Joe Johnston somewhere in his rear. He also dealt with a rival closer to home.

On May 30, Maj. Gen. John McClernand, commander of Grant's XIII Corps, circulated General Orders 72, which congratulated his men for their role in the May 22 attacks. Although the attacks failed, McClernand lauded his men's "constancy, valor, and success . . . the first and largest success achieved anywhere along the whole line of our army." In truth, his men had gained a small and temporary lodgment. McClernand blamed a lack of support from the rest of the army for his men's repulse.

McClernand forwarded this version of events to bolster the XIII Corps's morale, but more specifically, he intended it for the general public. As politician, McClernand had his eye on higher office, so he made sure his order not only circulated among his men but also appeared in a friendly newspaper. However, this violated a general order from Grant that prohibited official army correspondence from appearing in the press without authorization—an order intended to cut down on intelligence leaks.

Grant and McClernand had been butting heads since Fort Donelson, but Grant had been unable to rid himself of his troublesome subordinate because of McClernand's political value to Lincoln. Only after Grant had encircled Vicksburg had he amassed enough political capital of his own. Mid-campaign, Grant confirmed he had full authority to make personnel decisions within his command—Halleck, who disliked McClernand at least as much as Grant did, hid his derision in officious language.

Grant kept that approval in his pocket for just the right moment, in part because he didn't want to disrupt the command chain during active operations and in part because he waited for an opportunity clear-cut enough that McClernand's inevitable objections could be easily rebuffed. When McClernand's order appeared in the *Missouri Democrat* in violation of orders, Grant fired him, adding his own spin, "for his publication

TOP: **Dedicated on October 26, 1906, the Illinois State Memorial was designed by W. L. B. Jenney and sculpted by Charles J. Mulligan. The monument stands sixty-two feet in height and cost $194,423.92. It lists all 36,325 Illinois soldiers who participated in the Vicksburg Campaign—Grant most famous of all.** (cm)

LEFT: **Only Abraham Lincoln stands above Grant in the Illinois Memorial.** (cm)

of a congratulatory address calculated to create dissention and ill-feeling in the army."

Mostly, though, the siege left Grant bored—enough so that, on June 6, he decided to personally investigate rumors of a Confederate force up the Yazoo River near the town of Satartia, an area that could potentially serve as an avenue of advance for

Joe Johnston's rumored "Army of Relief." By the time Grant's steamboat arrived, a Confederate raid had driven Federal troops away, raising concerns about Grant's safety. Grant, though, was asleep in his cabin, so Charles Dana—assistant secretary of war and a former newspaper correspondent—ordered the boat back to Vicksburg.

As Dana later explained it, Grant was napping because he had become "as stupidly drunk as the immortal nature of man would allow." Other accounts suggest Grant was still getting over a bout of dysentery and had imbibed medicinal alcohol prescribed by his doctor. Unfortunately, the episode has haunted Grant ever since, with several versions of the story—written by people *not* on the trip—reaching outlandish proportions. As historian Timothy Smith has concluded, "there is no evidence that Grant or the army was ever in danger in the episode or that it was anything other than a little too much to drink for a general who was feeling ill and was on a boring steamboat trop amid what had become a boring siege at Vicksburg." As Dana himself observed, "the next day [Grant] came out as fresh as a rose."

\*   \*   \*

Siege operations brought the Federal army up to the Confederate works. The results of a pair of mine explosions on June 25 and July 1 convinced Grant that an all-out attack could breach the line. Federals could see for themselves how bedraggled Pemberton's starving troops had become. Grant set the assault for July 6.

But discontent inside Confederate lines would bring matters to a head sooner than that. "This army is now ripe for mutiny, unless it can be fed . . ." an anonymous note warned Pemberton. "[H]unger will compel a man to do almost anything." After surveying his division commanders, Pemberton finally admitted his army could neither break out or hold out. Joe Johnston, who kept sending puzzling messages to Pemberton, offered vague offers of assistance but no firm plan or guidance.

With all hope gone, Pemberton concluded, "[A] surrender with or without terms was the only alternative left to me."

On July 3, an aide arrived at Grant's tent. Confederates had sent an officer with a "proposition to save further effusion of blood. . . ."

Grant replied immediately: "The useless effusion of blood you propose stopping by this course can be ended at any time you may choose, by the unconditional surrender of the city and garrison. . . ."

Pemberton had chosen Maj. Gen. John Bowen to carry the message because Grant "knew him well and favorably before the war." Bowen now used his knowledge of both commanders to engineer a meeting between them, telling each—disingenuously—that the other wanted to meet.

At 3:00 that afternoon, Pemberton and Grant and two small clusters of officers met beneath an oak tree on a small knoll between the lines. As both commanders had arrived under false pretenses, the meeting soon became awkward.

"I understand that you expressed a wish to have a personal interview with me," Pemberton finally said.

*No,* Grant replied.

Pemberton turned to Bowen. "Then there is a misunderstanding," the commander said. "I certainly understood differently."

Grant said he was there for one reason only: "unconditional surrender of the city and garrison."

Maj. Gen. John Bowen, who knew Grant from St. Louis, carried Pemberton's initial surrender offer. He died of dysentery just days after Vicksburg's surrender. (loc)

No one overheard the conversation between Grant and Pemberton as they chit-chatted to the side while their staffs tried to hammer out a surrender agreement. (loc)

The oak tree under which Grant and Pemberton met vanished within 24 hours, chopped up for souvenirs. Soldiers from both sides even dug up the roots. (cm)

Frustrated, Pemberton turned to leave. "The conference might as well end," he snapped.

"Very well," Grant replied.

Trying to maintain his dignity, Pemberton blustered, "I can assure you, sir, you will bury many more of your men before you will enter Vicksburg."

Bowen again intervened, suggesting a conversation between the groups of subordinates. Grant agreed, and he and Pemberton stepped aside while the officers talked. The two generals sat beneath the oak, making small talk nobody overheard.

While the officers could not come to an arrangement, Grant said he would send a letter by 10:00 p.m. offering final terms. Pemberton, back at his headquarters, remained hopeful. "I am a Northern man; I know my people," said the Philadelphia native. "I know their peculiar weaknesses and their national vanity; I know we can get better terms from them on the 4th of July than any other day of the year. We must sacrifice ourselves to these considerations."

Grant ultimately called for Federal troops to occupy and guard the city. Officers were permitted to keep their side-arms, clothing, private baggage, and horses (if they owned one); enlisted men could keep their clothing but nothing else. Pemberton asked to change the terms so officers could keep their property, mor generally. Grant correctly saw that as a ruse for the officers to keep their enslaved servants, and he refused Pemberton's request. Federal victory meant emancipation.

At 10:00 a.m. on July 4, Pemberton's men marched out of the city, stacked arms, and retook their places in the works. Many "wept like children that all their long sacrifice was unavailing," one witness said. Grant's troops marched into Vicksburg and took possession of the city. Federals shared rations with starving Confederates, and everyone settled into the business of occupation. Grant would eventually parole Pemberton's men, knowing that if he took them prisoner, the logistics of transporting them north from Vicksburg "would have used all the transportation we had for a month."

As Grant's army filtered into the city, the general himself rode down to the river to meet Porter, where the navy was just as abuzz as the army. "There was one man there who preserved the same quiet demeanor he always bore, whether in adversity or in victory, and that was General Grant," Porter later recollected. "No one, to see him sitting there with that calm exterior amid all the jollity, and without any staff, would ever have taken him for the great general who had accomplished one of the most stupendous military feats on record. There was a quiet satisfaction in his face that could not be concealed, but he behaved on that occasion as if nothing of importance had occurred."

Celebratory officers offered him a drink, but according to Porter, "Grant was the only one in that assemblage who did not touch the simple wine offered him; he contented himself with a cigar."

*Chattanooga*

CHAPTER NINE

*July–December 1863*

News of Vicksburg's surrender didn't reach President Lincoln until July 7. In the interim period, the president found himself on July 5 talking with Maj. Gen. Dan Sickles, a Union officer who'd been seriously wounded at the battle of Gettysburg on July 3. Much of the conversation focused on Sickles's slanted perspective of the fight in Pennsylvania, but at one point, the flow of the conversation switched to Mississippi. Grant, the president said, "does not worry and bother me. He isn't shrieking for reinforcements all the time. He takes what troops we can safely give him . . . and does the best he can with what he has got." Lincoln then offered an endorsement of his western general that would prove prescient: "And if Grant only does this thing down there, I don't care much how, so long as he does it right—why, Grant is my man and I am his the rest of the war!"

It would take some time for Lincoln to put his promise into action, though. In the meantime, Grant would languish through yet another Halleck-induced period of limbo.

"[T]he troops that had done so much should be allowed to do more before the enemy could recover from the blow he had received," Grant decided, "and

**With Lookout Mountain looming the background, Grant inspected the river crossing at Brown's Ferry—the first step in opening "the Cracker Line" to resupply the besieged Federal army.** (ac/cf)

while important points might be captured without bloodshed." He set his sights on Mobile, Alabama— an objective the navy had been targeting since the fall of New Orleans in the spring of 1862. The only Confederate force that could impede such a move was Braxton Bragg's army outside Chattanooga, Tennessee, but if Bragg moved to intercept, that would leave William Rosecrans's Army of the Cumberland free for an unimpeded move into Georgia.

However, Henry Halleck's jealousy of Grant apparently flared up once again. Rather than green-light Grant's plan, Halleck began detailing parts of Grant's army to widely scattered assignments. "The General-in-chief having decided against me, the depletion of an army, which had won a succession of great victories, commenced . . ." Grant lamented. He later noted, perhaps as a satisfied "I told you so," that "All these movements came to naught."

One of the detachments went to New Orleans to—finally—bolster Nathaniel Banks's force. Grant received orders to assist. During his time in the Crescent City, Grant reviewed Banks's army, and on the way back, had a severe accident. "The horse I rode was vicious and but little used," he explained. A locomotive came by the group and the engineer recognized Grant and laid down on the whistle, spooking the horse, Charlie, who fell, "probably on me." Grant was unsure exactly what happened because the fall rendered him "insensible," but when he regained consciousness, he found himself in a hotel surrounded by doctors. "My leg was swollen from the knee to the thigh, and the swelling, almost to the point of bursting, extended along the body up to the armpit," he recalled. "The pain was almost beyond endurance."

It took weeks to recover. Grant passed the time by reading a favorite book, *Phoenixiana*, by a West Point classmate, George H. Derby, writing under the pen name of John Phoenix. Grant also kept in close consultation with Sherman back in Vicksburg, who refused to take command in Grant's stead. "It would confuse the records," said Sherman, who let all orders be made in Grant's name.

On September 16, Grant received the first indication of a problem in East Tennessee: Halleck ordered him to send troops there as quickly as possible. Over the next couple of weeks, Grant began shuffling divisions to meet the growing crisis.

On September 18, the Army of the Cumberland ran into trouble along Chickamauga Creek in northwest Georgia. Defeated, the army retreated back to Chattanooga, where Bragg's Confederates bottled them up. Grant remained unclear on all the details of the aftermath, but in early October, he received orders to mobilize to help meet the emergency—summoned first to Cairo, Illinois, then to Louisville, Kentucky. "I was still very lame," Grant admitted, "but started without delay."

According to Grant, Edwin Stanton "cared nothing for the feeling of others. In fact it seemed to be pleasanter to him to disappoint than to gratify." Grant did call him "an able constitutional lawyer and jurist" but "a man who never questioned his own authority, and who always did in war time what he wanted to do." (loc)

\*    \*    \*

Grant's trip enabled him to reunite with Julia and their children, who accompanied him on his trip to Louisville. The train took him by way of Indianapolis. There, an unnamed representative of the War Department intercepted him for a top-secret meeting.

The official was none other than the secretary of war, Edwin Stanton.

The two men had corresponded frequently over the previous year via telegraph, but they had never met in person. Upon entering the train car, Stanton rushed over, all handshakes and platitudes: "General Grant! It's so good to meet you! I'd know you anywhere! Yes, sir, it's so good to meet you!" Except the person Stanton had latched on to was Grant's surgeon, Dr. Edward Kittoe, similarly bearded as Grant. When Stanton finally stopped pumping the doctor's hand, Kittoe gestured across the car to Grant, who was leaning on a cabinet, enjoying the scene. "I'm not Grant," the doctor said. "That's Grant."

Stanton hardly skipped a beat. Turning to Grant, he rushed over and grasped the general's hand. "General Grant! It's so good to meet you! I'd know you anywhere!"

The men got down to business as the train moved south. Stanton produced two sets of papers from an inner coat pocket. "You must make your choice of them," Stanton said. "They are identical in all but one particular." Both placed Grant in charge of all Federal troops between the Allegheny Mountains

Grant first met Andrew Johnson, Military Governor of Tennessee, while on his way to Chattanooga. Johnson "delivered a speech of welcome. His composure showed that it was by no means his maiden effort. It was long, and I was in torture while he was delivering it. . . ." (loc)

Grant considered "Fighting Joe" Hooker "a dangerous man. He was not subordinate to his superiors. He was ambitious to the extent of caring nothing for the rights of others." (loc)

and the Mississippi River; one left the department commanders as they were, while the other replaced Rosecrans with Maj. Gen. George Thomas. "I accepted the later," Grant later stated.

Grant never bothered to explain his choice. It's possible that, having suffered a major loss at Chickamauga and then letting his army get bottled in Chattanooga, Rosecrans no longer held Washington's confidence, as evidenced by the pre-prepared orders, and that was enough for Grant. It's also possible that Grant saw an opportunity to preemptively relieve himself of a man who had already proven himself to be a problematic subordinate.

By October 20, Grant was on his way from Louisville to Nashville and then on to Chattanooga. Reports of severe supply shortages prompted Grant to write ahead to George Thomas: Hold on. Thomas immediately responded, "We will hold the town till we starve."

Grant's route took him through Stevenson Alabama, where he intersected with Rosecrans, then heading to the rear for reassignment. "Old Rosey" met with Grant for "a brief interview," during which time "he described very clearly the situation at Chattanooga, and made some excellent suggestions as to what should be done." Grant's only wonder was why Rosecrans had not carried them out.

Grant also met two other new subordinates, Maj. Gens. Oliver Otis Howard and Joseph "Fighting Joe" Hooker, both recently transferred with reinforcements to the Western Theater from the Army of the Potomac. Howard came to see Grant at once, but Hooker sent a staff officer with an invitation for Grant to join him at his headquarters. "If General Hooker wishes to see me, he will find me on this train," Grant replied. "The answer and the manner of it surprised me," Howard admitted, "but it was Grant's way of maintaining his ascendency. . . ." Hooker soon showed himself to pay his respects.

The final leg of the trip to Chattanooga was by horseback. "[T]he roads were almost impassable from mud, knee-deep in places, and from wash-outs on the mountain sides," Grant recalled. "The roads were strewn with the debris of broken wagons and the carcasses of thousands of starved mules and horses."

In places, even the horses couldn't get through and Grant—still on crutches—had to be carried. At one point, Grant's horse, Jack, stumbled in the mud and fell, tossing Grant onto his injured left side. The soft mud cushioned most of the blow.

It was after dark, and in a chilling rain, when Grant arrived in Chattanooga, "wet, dirty, and well." He went directly to Thomas's headquarters, a plain wooden, one-story dwelling on Walnut Street. There, staff officer James H. Wilson found Grant warming himself by the fireplace, "steaming from the heat over a small puddle which had run from his sodden clothing. Thomas was on the other side, neither saying a word, but both looking glum and ill at ease."

Other officers arrived and took places in the room, summoned by Thomas for an initial meeting with the new commander. "How do you do!" Grant said to each of them in a low voice, slowly, framing his greeting as a statement rather than a question. With a lit cigar in his mouth, Grant took a seat among them, stooping slightly, with his head bent slightly forward.

Wilson, meanwhile, quietly pointed out to Thomas that Grant remained wet and muddy. "This broke the silence and set the machinery of hospitality in motion," Wilson recounted. "It had apparently not occurred to the stately Virginian that Grant was his guest as well as his commanding general. . . ." Thomas roused himself to offer Grant a change of

"Coming to us crowned with the laurels he had gained in the brilliant campaign of Vicksburg, we naturally expected to meet a well-equipped soldier, but hardly anybody was prepared to find one who had the grasp, the promptness of decision, and the general administrative capacity which he displayed at the very start as commander of an extensive military division, in which many complicated problems were presented for immediate solution." (cwg)

"'Old Pap Thomas,' as we all loved to call him, was more of a father than a commander to the younger officers who served under his immediate command, and he possessed their warmest affections," wrote young Horace Porter of Maj. Gen. George Thomas, commander of the Army of the Cumberland. (loc)

Phil Sheridan's fighting spirit made an immediate positive impression on Grant, and that esteem would only grow as they worked together over time. "I believe General Sheridan has no superior as a general, either living or dead, and perhaps not an equal," Grant would eventually say. (loc)

uniform and supper; Grant accepted the meal but declined the dry clothes.

Historians have subsequently made much of "Thomas's coolness and neglect," as Wilson described it. Some ascribe it to jealousy on Thomas's part while others point to Thomas's loyalty to Rosecrans and a subsequent resentment of Grant. All interpretations are colored by the complex but cordial relationship that Grant and Thomas shared. "On the whole Grant spoke very favorably of Thomas," historian Frank Varney writes, "yet he successfully painted him as slow and deliberate: an image which has persisted to this day."

As the opening engagement in that complicated relationship, historians have often interpreted the first meeting at Chattanooga more like an opening salvo. If the meeting bothered Grant at all, he made no mention of it in his memoirs, glossing over the event entirely. Eventual Grant staffer Horace Porter—who met Grant for the first time that night—probably interprets the meeting most accurately: "General Thomas's mind had been so intent upon receiving the commander, and arranging for a conference of officers, that he had entirely overlooked his guest's travel-stained condition." Porter credits Thomas for "his old-time Virginia hospitality" once Wilson offered his tactful reminder, and even Wilson admitted "Everything possible was done and apparently in the most cheerful manner to make Grant and his staff comfortable."

Thomas's officers took turns offering their take on events at Chattanooga while Grant sat "as immovable as a rock and as silent as the sphinx, but listened attentively to all that was said." Once everyone had their say, "he began to fire whole volleys of questions at the officers present." His queries demonstrated a full grasp of events.

By the next evening—after a personal inspection of the Federal position—Grant scribbled out order after order after order. "[H]e tossed the sheets of paper across the table as he finished them, leaving them in the wildest disorder," observed Porter, on hand at Grant's request. "When he had completed the despatch, he gathered up the scattered sheets, read them over rapidly, and arranged them in their proper order."

"Their execution . . ." historian William S. McFeely succinctly wrote, "created the campaign that routed Braxton Bragg."

\* \* \*

Under Grant's firm hand, the Army of the Cumberland established a new supply line for itself—the "Cracker Line," as it has come to be known, named after the hard tack that served as a staple of a soldier's diet. Rosecrans had already laid out a plan for opening a supply line but, inexplicably, had not implemented it. Instead, Brig. Gen. William F. "Baldy" Smith presented the plan to Grant, claiming it as its own. Grant immediately agreed.

The operation began on the army's left flank, threatened by Confederate Lt. Gen. James Longstreet. An old and dear friend of Grant's, Longstreet commanded the First Corps of the Army of Northern Virginia, which had been sent on detached duty to help Bragg's Army of Tennessee. Longstreet's men had proven to be the decisive factor in the Confederate victory at Chickamauga. Longstreet and Bragg did not get along, though, and their squabbling threw Longstreet off his game. On the evening of October 27, Federals secured a small victory against Longstreet's men at Brown's Ferry, then beat back a feeble counterattack the next day at Wauhatchie. The successes improved the flow of food, clothing, and medical supplies to the Army of the Cumberland.

"The men were soon reclothed and also well fed," Grant later reported; "an abundance of ammunition was brought up, and a cheerfulness prevailed not before enjoyed in many weeks. Neither officers nor men looked upon themselves any longer as doomed."

As the army regained its strength, Grant looked to other parts of his command. Hooker and Howard occupied positions to keep the new supply line secure. Major General Ambrose Burnside occupied Union-friendly east Tennessee around Knoxville. Sherman approached from Corinth, Mississippi. The combined forces put tremendous stress on an already inadequate railroad, so Grant ordered a detail to begin repairs and the construction of new lines.

Horace Porter, who would go on to play an important role in Grant's miliary family, recorded his first impression of Grant as "a general officer, slight in figure and of medium stature, whose face bore an expression of weariness." (loc)

James H. Wilson considered Grant "altogether the most thoughtful and considerate general with whom I ever served in regard to the comfort of his staff and of the troops under his command." (loc)

On one occasion, Grant rode down to the banks of Chattanooga Creek, which separated the two armies on the Federal left flank. The men there, according to Porter, "had established a temporary truce on their own responsibility, and the men of each army were allowed to get water from the same stream without being fired upon by those on the other side." Grant thought he might be able to approach the banks alone without attracting much attention, but one Federal picket, recognizing him, called out the customary, "Turn out the guard—commanding general!"

Grant growled, "Never mind the guard!"

His caution did no good, though, because on the far bank, a Confederate picket station of about 20 men—in full view and within easy range—played along. "Turn out the guard for the commanding general—General Grant!" a sentinel called. Confederates then promptly formed up, facing the Federal position on the far bank, and presented arms. Amused, Grant saluted them by lifting his hat before riding on.

*    *    *

Aside from the newly gained ground on the Federal left, the Confederate position nearly encircled Grant's forces in Chattanooga. Confederates held a stronghold atop Lookout Mountain that dominated the landscape from the southwest; on the east, Missionary Ridge, "about two hundred feet high, fortified by rifle trenches at top and bottom" hemmed Federals in, and, said James Wilson, "regarded as secure against direct attack" because of its steep slopes. The Tennessee River—which had done so much for Grant at Fort Henry and Shiloh—now served as an obstruction, preventing Federals from retreating north.

"Why, General Grant, you are besieged," Sherman observed upon his arrival.

"It is too true," Grant replied.

To break out of this trap, Grant devised a plan for Sherman to attack the Confederate right flank on the north tip of Missionary Ridge. Meanwhile, Thomas would demonstrate against the center of the Ridge to prevent those Confederates from shifting as reinforcements. Hooker was to target Lookout Mountain and threaten the Confederate left.

After some shuffling and false starts—and the departure of Longstreet toward Burnside in Knoxville—Grant set his plan in motion.

On November 23, Federal forces captured an advance post called Orchard Knob, midway between the city and the foot of Missionary Ridge. On November 24, Hooker captured Lookout Mountain in a fight that became known as "The Battle Above the Clouds." The next day, Sherman and Thomas launched their attacks on Missionary Ridge, with Hooker ordered to put pressure on the Confederate left.

Grant watched the action from the top of Orchard Knob. "The morning of the 25th opened clear and bright, and the whole field was in full view," he wrote. He could even see Bragg's headquarters atop Missionary Ridge, with officers coming and going constantly.

A monument to Illinois soldiers, designed by George Craig and dedicated in 1899, stands atop Orchard Knob today. (cm)

By midafternoon, it became apparent that Sherman had bogged down, and Grant ordered Thomas to begin his demonstration. After some delay, Thomas's men went forward. Grant expected them to stop at a line of Confederate rifle pits along the base of the ridge but, pinned down as they were by fire coming down on them from the ridge above, they realized their only hope of relief was to continue the attack. As they pushed up the slope, Grant—back on Orchard Knob—asked Thomas and the gaggle of officers around them, "Who ordered that attack?"

"I don't know," replied Thomas. "*I* did not."

One of Thomas's corps commanders, Maj. Gen. Gordon Granger, chimed in. "When those fellows get started, all hell can't stop them," he said.

Grant tried at first to countermand the attack, but the momentum of the spontaneous attack took

Federals to the crest of the ridge, pushing Bragg's men off. Bragg's entire army soon fell back into Georgia.

"The victory at Chattanooga was won against great odds, considering the advantage the enemy had of position, and was accomplished more easily than was expected . . ." Grant summarized years later. He claimed in his memoirs that the battle was fought exactly as he had originally planned, but in fact, Chattanooga consisted of a variety of improvisations, from Hooker's capture of Lookout Mountain to Thomas's capture of Missionary Ridge. Even the opening of the Cracker Line depended on leftover plans from Rosecrans.

But Grant did have legitimate reasons to be proud of the victory. "In the battle of Chattanooga, troops from the Army of the Potomac, from the Army of the Tennessee, and from the Army of the Cumberland participated," he noted, which represented his orchestrated use of an army group. His strategic vision continued to develop and, most crucially, his basic tenacity once again paid off. While the victory did not destroy Bragg's army, it did lead to Bragg's eventual replacement, and it opened the way for Sherman's 1864 Atlanta campaign.

Historian William McFeely, in his Pulitzer Prize-winning biography, *Grant*, suggested "the engagement may even have been the turning point of the war." Grant himself certainly gave it much weight: when asked to write about his wartime exploits for the *Century Magazine* in 1885—a project that would evolve into his memoirs—Grant chose Chattanooga as one of his four topics, swapping out an agreed-upon article about Appomattox Court House to make room.

As he had done after Vicksburg, President Lincoln sent Grant a gracious note: "I wish to tender you, and all under your command, my more than thanks—my profound gratitude—for the skill, courage, and perseverance, with which you and they, over so great difficulties, have effected that important object. God bless you all."

**Following the battle, Grant (left) climbed to the top of Lookout Mountain for a look of his own. John Rawlins is the seated man furthest to the left.** (loc)

# *Lieutenant General*

## CHAPTER TEN
### *March 1864*

On his initial journey into Chattanooga, during his stop in Stevenson, Alabama, Grant had shared "a fair sunrise breakfast" with Maj. Gen. O. O. Howard before continuing on his way. During their conversation, Grant made a comment that "impressed me at the time more than I can explain," Howard later recalled. Grant said, "If I should seek a command higher than that entrusted to me by my government, I should be flying in the face of Providence."

Grant's subsequent success at Chattanooga provided the government with an opportunity to entrust him with higher command.

Lincoln had already pledged Grant as his man following the capture of Vicksburg, but he needed to see if he was Grant's man. Lincoln's political fate seemed uncertain as 1863 came to a close, and he did not necessarily want to elevate Grant to a position that would, in turn, make Grant a rival for the presidency in the 1864 election. Through intermediaries, Lincoln made discreet inquiries. Grant—unaware of Lincoln's concerns—categorically dismissed the idea. "I already have a pretty big job on my hands, and my only ambition is to see this rebellion suppressed," Grant told one of the intermediaries. "Nothing would

"I think I should have failed in this position if I had come to it in the beginning," Grant later admitted, "because I should not have had confidence enough." (ac/cf)

induce me to think of being a presidential candidate, particularly so long as there is a possibility of having Mr. Lincoln re-elected."

And so it was, in December, that Grant's patron in the House, Elihu Washburne, introduced HR 26, which resurrected the rank of lieutenant general, a rank only ever held by George Washington. (Winfield Scott held the rank as a brevet, but Congress never made it permanent.) Senator James Doolittle of Wisconsin sponsored similar legislation in the Senate. The House bill specifically named Grant for the post; the Senate bill did not.

Washburne crowed that Grant had "captured more prisoners and taken more guns than any general in modern times." Indeed, only two Confederate armies had surrendered during the war, both to Grant. No other Union general could claim even one.

Debate on the bill continued through February, and Lincoln made his support known. The House finally passed its version 117 to 19; the Senate version, with Grant's name omitted, passed 31 to 6. Opponents generally argued that Lincoln already had the authority he needed to name a general in chief and so did not need new legislation, and some thought the prestigious rank should be given after the war as a reward for service. "Saints are not canonized until after death," grumbled Pennsylvania Congressman Thaddeus Stevens, who opposed the measure.

On February 29, the reconciled measure passed, and a clerk brought the legislation from the capitol to the White House, as was customary. But as the clerk turned to leave, Lincoln asked him to wait a moment. The president stopped what he was doing and signed the legislation on the spot, adding, "I nominate Ulysses S. Grant, now a Major General in the military service, to be Lieutenant General in the Army of the United States."

After the preceding months' debate, the nomination came as no surprise, and the Senate confirmed the president's recommendation on March 2. On March 3, Halleck—about to be supplanted as general in chief—sent Grant a telegram ordering him to "report in person to the War Dept as early as practicable considering the condition of your command."

Washburne had tipped Grant off to events. Grant placed Sherman in charge before he left. "Whilst I have been eminently successful in this War . . ." he told his friend and lieutenant, "what I want is to express my thanks to you and McPherson as *the men* to whom, above all others, I feel indebted for whatever I have had of success." He praised their energy, skill, and harmonious working relationship.

In acknowledging Grant's "more than kind and characteristic letter," Sherman mixed warmth and warning. "You are now [George] Washington's legitimate successor and occupy a position of almost dangerous elevation," Sherman wrote, "but if you can continue heretofore to be yourself, simple, honest, and unpretending, you will enjoy through life the respect and love of friends, and the homage of millions. . . ."

"We have done much," Sherman added, "but still much remains to be done."

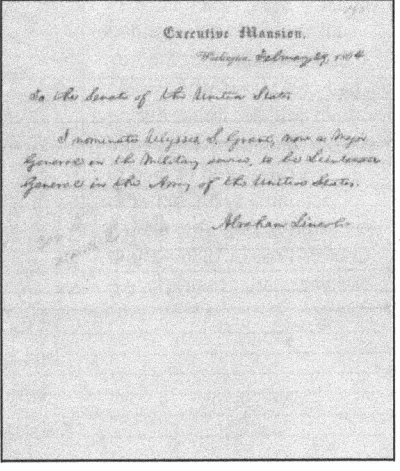

**When Lincoln signed into law the legislation that created the rank of lieutenant general, he immediately scribbled out a nomination for U. S. Grant to fill the role.** (loc)

\* \* \*

Grant arrived in the capital on March 8, his 14-year-old son, Fred, in tow, along with staffers John Rawlins and Cyrus Comstock and Brig. Gen. "Baldy" Smith from the Army of the Cumberland. Grant left his entourage to their own devices, but as was his duty, he called on Halleck to pay his respects. Finding him not at the War Department nor at home, Grant felt he had done his due diligence and finally went to his hotel to check in.

The Willard Hotel, around the block from the White House, served as the informal center of Washington's political world. Politicians and power brokers hob-knobbed, looked for opportunities, pitched ideas, and struck deals. Grant—in his plain linen duster, worn and faded, over his traveling uniform—might have seemed out of place but took no notice. The clerk at the desk, meanwhile, seemed to barely take notice of Grant, dismissing him to a small, top-floor room. "That would be fine," Grant said, signing the ledger: "U. S. Grant and son, Galena, IL."

**Cyrus Comstock earned Grant's respect while working as an engineer overseeing aspects of the Vicksburg siege. When Grant came east, he brought Comstock with him to serve on the general staff.** (loc)

Fred Grant suffered a near-fatal case of Typhoid fever in January 1864, which doctors attributed to an extended case of dysentery the boy had contracted while in the field with his father during the Vicksburg campaign. He recovered in time to accompany his father to Washington, D.C. This sketch depicts Fred in 1866—about two years after their trip. (loc)

Seeing the signature, the clerk immediately realized his unfortunate error. Apologizing profusely, he quickly reassigned Grant to Parlor 6, one of the best suites in the hotel—the same room Lincoln had stayed in before his inauguration. Now Grant, too, was about to ascend to a higher office.

As porters took Grant's minimal luggage to the suite, Grant took Fred to the dining room. Their comfortable anonymity did not last long. A congressman recognized them and stood to offer a toast: "Ladies and gentlemen, I present to you Lieutenant General Ulysses S. Grant!" Well-wishers, autograph seekers, and glad-handers of all sorts mobbed the general as he and his son tried to eat.

After escaping the crush, Grant took Fred back to the room and then set out for the White House. The Lincolns were holding their weekly public reception, and the president had asked Grant to stop by. Unable to change out of his worn uniform—Grant couldn't find the key to his travel trunk—he went to the reception as-is. Comstock and Rawlins tagged along. They arrived at the Executive Mansion around 9:30 p.m.

Word that Grant might attend the reception had drawn a huge crowd, but the president and the general found each other quickly. Lincoln's height dominated the crowd, making him easy for Grant to spot. Lincoln, meanwhile, had prepped for the meeting by studying pictures of Grant in advance and so recognized him immediately.

"Why here is General Grant! Well, this is a great pleasure, I assure you," the president said, grasping his hand.

After a few moments of introductions to Mrs. Lincoln and other dignitaries in the reception line and the crowd gathering around them, Lincoln asked Secretary of State William Seward to direct Grant into the adjacent, larger East Room. "Grant! Grant! Grant!" the crowd chanted. The throng pressed so close that the general eventually had to stand on a sofa—against his better judgment, knowing that his wife would have objected to dusty boots on the furniture. He also feared what Mrs. Lincoln might think of him. Yet even she was won over by Grant's quiet, deferential manner that evening.

"He blushed like a girl," a reporter noted. "The handshaking brought streams of perspiration down his forehead and over his face." The ordeal lasted an hour before Grant finally slipped away with Lincoln and Seward for some time alone.

The formal conferral of the lieutenant generalcy would take place the following day, and, as Grant recalled, "knowing my disinclination to speak in public, [the president] handed me a copy in advance so that I might prepare a few lines of reply." Lincoln even offered a couple pointers on what Grant might possibly say. Perhaps, he suggested, Grant could say something that might soothe the Army of the Potomac, which had taken abuse from the Army of

**Understanding the symbolic importance of the moment, Grant prepared comments for the formal acceptance of his commission to lieutenant general. (hw)**

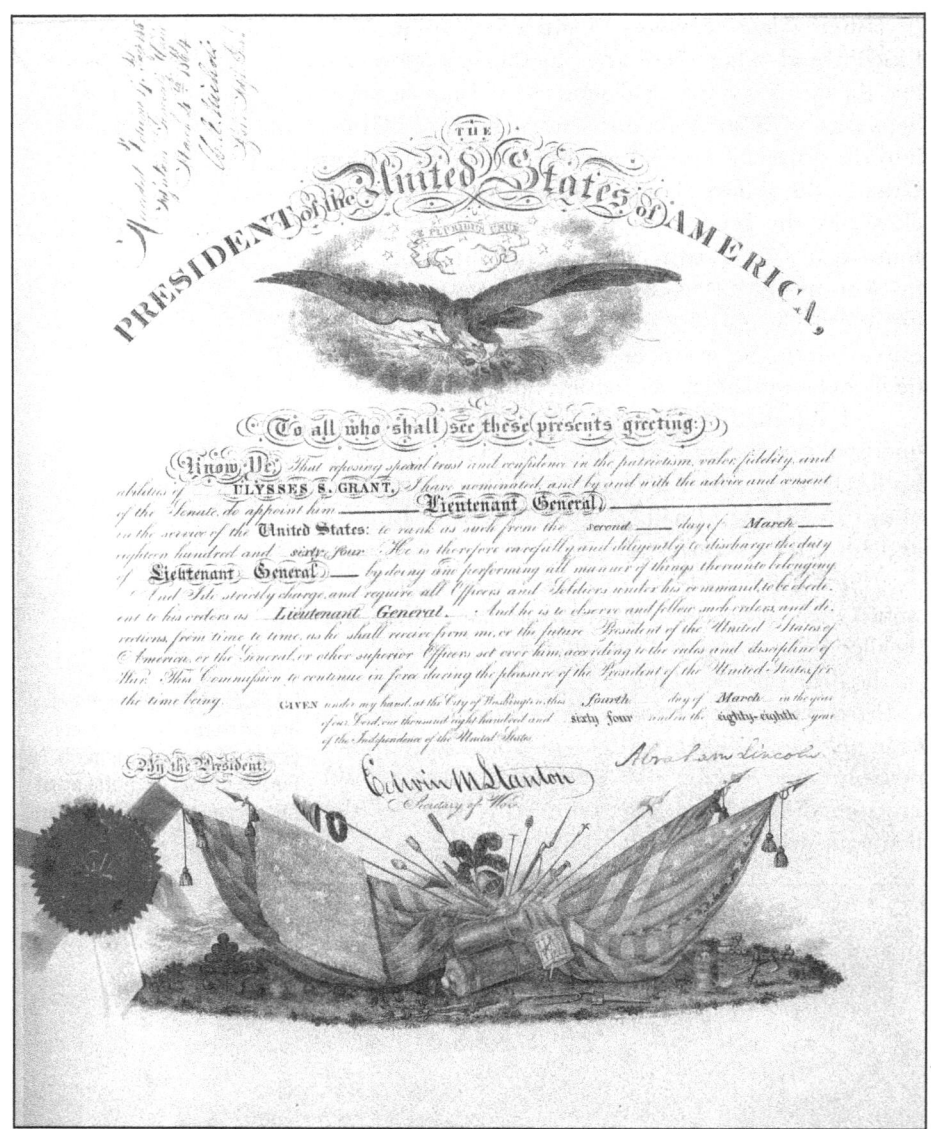

**Grant's commission to lieutenant general has been on display in the Smithsonian Museum of American History.** (loc)

Northern Virginia for well over a year and a half and might see Grant's arrival as a reprimand. Lincoln also suggested that Grant try to soothe the officer corps.

Lincoln's cabinet met the following morning, with Halleck in attendance, along with a few guests. Grant brought his entourage of Fred, Rawlins, and Comstock. Lincoln read his prepared remarks and, in presenting the commission, reminded Grant, "With this high honor devolves upon you also, a corresponding responsibility."

Grant understood the gravity of the charge placed on him, but an unexpected weight to the moment caught him off guard. He'd written his brief response on a scrap of paper at the Willard and tucked it into a pocket, but he suddenly couldn't find it. When he did, he seemed to have trouble deciphering his own pencil scratches. But then his nerves settled, and he spoke:

*Mr. President, I accept the Commission with gratitude for the high honor conferred. With the aid of the noble armies that have fought in so many fields for our common country, it will be my earnest endeavor not to disappoint your expectations. I feel the full weight of the responsibilities now devolving on me and know that if they are met, it will be due to those armies, and, above all to the favor of that Providence which leads both Nations and men.*

Grant's comments reflected the same mindset he had articulated in his March 4 letter to Sherman: his success, if he had any, would come from the men who served under him.

Yet Grant deliberately omitted the reassurances to those men that Lincoln had suggested the previous evening. To some degree, Grant's omission reflected his personal aversion to flattery and ego-stroking. He knew actions spoke louder than words. Soon enough, the proof would be in the pudding, as it were, and there was no boast he could make or reassurance he could offer that would make it otherwise.

And hadn't generals George McClellan, John Pope, and Joe Hooker all ascended to command with bold and pompous predictions only to eat crow after Robert E. Lee humiliated them on the battlefield? Grant would not set himself up for similar embarrassment.

Grant's omissions were also a show of independence from his new boss. Lincoln had told Grant he would defer to Grant's way of doing things, and Grant had, in this small way, tested him on that pledge. Lincoln, if he minded, never said a word— passing an important test through his silence.

\*     \*     \*

Maj. Gen. William F. "Baldy" Smith showed talent on the battlefield, but he was a constant troublemaker with his superiors. His inability to get along sabotaged his otherwise promising military career on more than one occasion. Having once already been banished from the Army of the Potomac, had he been placed in army command in 1864, it would have stirred old animosities. (loc)

The next day saw heavy rain. Grant boarded a train to Culpeper Court House, 70 miles southwest of Washington along the Orange & Alexandria Railroad. There, the Army of the Potomac had made winter quarters opposite the Army of Northern Virginia, ensconced on the far bank of the Rapidan River around Orange Court House.

Despite the rain, an honor guard of brightly colored Zouaves, with baggy pants and red fezzes, met Grant at the train station. So did Brig. Gen. Andrew A. Humphreys, the Army of the Potomac's irascible but highly capable chief of staff. Army commander George Gordon Meade was sick with a cold, he explained, but Humphreys would take Grant directly to him.

Among Grant's small entourage was "Baldy" Smith—a possible candidate for army command. Smith had served with the army previously but had been transferred away as part of a shake-up in the early winter of 1863. But Grant—who had come to trust Smith through their time together in Chattanooga— saw that previous service with the Army of the Potomac as a crucial component of credibility. In the wake of Grant's capture of Vicksburg, Grant's name had circulated as a possible candidate to take command of the Army of the Potomac, but Grant dismissed the idea for a variety of reasons, one of which was his status as an "outsider" from the West. "Dissatisfaction would necessarily be produced by importing a General to command an Army already well supplied with those who have grown up, and been promoted, with it," he told Charles Dana. He was still sensitive to that dynamic now—and freshly reminded of it by Lincoln in the friendly suggestions he had ignored for his acceptance speech.

As a result, Humphreys noted, the visit took on the feel of "the visit of a rival commander to a rival army, or at least the meeting of the commanders and officers of rival armies."

Meade, for his part, greeted Grant warmly, shaking his hand before Grant even dismounted from his horse. They had met briefly, long ago in the Mexican War, but otherwise didn't know each other, but their conversation quickly became "cordial and demonstrative," Humphreys said. Meade invited

Grant into his tent for a conversation both men anticipated and, perhaps a little, dreaded.

Meade cut to the chase, politely but bluntly. "You might want an officer who has served with you in the West to take my place," he said. "If so, do not hesitate about making the change. The work before us is of such vast importance to the whole nation that the feeling or wishes of no one person should stand in the way of selecting the right men for all positions. For myself, I will serve to the best of my ability wherever placed."

As Grant later explained, "This incident gave me even a more favorable opinion of Meade than did his great victory at Gettysburg the July before. It is men who wait to be selected, and not those who seek, from whom we may always expect the most efficient service." He might well have been articulating his own philosophy about power and advancement.

Meade left the meeting feeling equally impressed. Grant "showed much more capacity and character than I had expected," he wrote to his wife. In a subsequent letter, he said Grant was "so much more active than his predecessor [Halleck], and agrees so well with me in his views, I cannot but be rejoiced at his arrival, because I believe success to be the more probable. . . . My duty is plain, to continue quietly to discharge my duties, heartily co-operating with him and under him."

The only point of concern for Meade was Grant's decision to make his headquarters in the field rather than in the capital. Grant had originally expected to return to the field in the West, but "when I got to Washington and saw the situation it was plain that here was the point for the commanding general to be," he realized. Meade immediately understood the shadow Grant would cast. "[L]ook for the army of the Potomac putting laurels on the brow of another rather than your husband," he conceded to his wife, but added later, "Cheerfully I will give him all credit if he can bring the war to a close."

Meade downplayed these concerns—sometimes sounding a little like he was whistling past the graveyard as he did so—but Grant himself "tried to make General Meade's position as nearly as possible what it would have been if I had been in Washington or any other place away from his command." All

According to Grant, George Gordon Meade "was certainly among the heroes of the war, and his name deserves all honor. I had a great fondness for him. No general ever was more earnest. As a commander in the field, he had only one fault — his temper. . . . Under this harsh exterior Meade had a gentle, chivalrous heart, and was an accomplished soldier and gentleman." The relationship between Grant and Meade was vital to final victory in the war, yet it has remained one of the most understudied—and baffling—of Grant's key relationships. (loc)

**Grant and Sherman met in person for one final time before the spring campaigns got underway. Sherman urged Grant to stay in the west—and as far away from Washington, D.C., as possible.** (loc)

orders for the army went through Meade, who soon realized with more than a hint of appreciation that "Grant is emphatically an executive man, whose only place is in the field. . . ."

Meade eventually came to perhaps regret that last statement. Grant's presence with the Army of the Potomac would put Meade in the exact situation Halleck had placed Grant in the weeks following Shiloh when Grant languished in administrative obscurity. As Grant later admitted, "Meade's position afterwards proved embarrassing to me if not to him."

*     *     *

"Grant, who at Chattanooga thought Baldy Smith should have it, now says no change," Comstock noted in his diary. "The programme is, Halleck here as office man and military adviser, Sherman to take Grant's place, McPherson Sherman's, Grant in the field." John Logan would ascend to command of McPherson's corps.

Grant returned to Washington only long enough to catch a train west so he could confer in person with Sherman. Lincoln first tried to cajole his new lieutenant general into attending a dinner at the White House, but Grant demurred. "Really, Mr. President, I have had enough of this show business," he admitted. He had much to do and much on his mind, and he wanted nothing more than to get to work.

Sherman's words—"We have done much, but still much remains to be done"—no doubt rang in his ears.

# The Wilderness

## CHAPTER ELEVEN
### *April–May 1864*

By mid-May 1864, with a brutal campaign underway through the heart of Virginia, Grant pulled troops from the garrisons around Washington, D.C. to reinforce the Army of the Potomac. Secretary of War Stanton balked. Grant calmly maintained that he had the authority to reassign the troops. *We'll see about that*, Stanton growled—and took the matter to the president.

"You and I, Mr. Stanton, have been trying to boss this job," Lincoln told him, "and we have not succeeded very well with it. We have sent across the mountain for Mr. Grant, as Mrs. Grant calls him, to relieve us, and I think we had better leave him alone to do as he pleases."

Lincoln had not shown a similar hands-off attitude toward any of his other generals thus far in the war. As a commander in chief, Lincoln had matured, but Grant had also earned his confidence in a way other generals had not. "Stoddard, Grant is the first general I've had!" Lincoln told his secretary one day. "He's a general!"

As Grant later explained, the president "had never professed to be a military man or to know how campaigns should be conducted, and never wanted to

Dressed in their civilian clothes, Curt Fields and Thomas Jessee vist the Brock Road/Plank Road intersection in the Wilderness, the battlefield where their counterparts, Grant and Lee, first met. The intersection was a literal and figurative crossroad in Grant's career and in the course of the war. (cm)

interfere in them. . . . All he wanted or had ever wanted was some one who would take the responsibility and act, and call on him for all the assistance needed, pledging himself to use all the power of the government in rendering such assistance."

"[H]e did not care to know what I was to do, only to know what I wanted; that I should have all I required," Grant added. "He wished me to beat Lee, how I did it was my own duty. He said he did not wish to know my plans or to exercise any scrutiny over my plans; so long as I beat the rebel army he was satisfied."

Grant assured Lincoln, "I will do the best I can with the means at hand, and avoid as far as possible annoying you or the War Department." Beyond that, he communicated with Washington as necessary but otherwise kept his own counsel on strategy within the broad parameters Lincoln had set.

This would become a matter of personal policy for Grant, who would not only have to contend with Confederate armies but with a flurry of official busybodies from Washington making constant visits. He had not had to contend with such nuisance out west, but proximity to the nation's capital made it unavoidable. Staffer Horace Porter said Grant adopted a philosophical attitude: "the unspoken word is a sword in the scabbard, while the spoken word is a sword in the hand of one's enemy."

"When questioned beyond the bounds of propriety, his lips closed like a vise, and the obtruding party was left to supply all the subsequent conversation," Porter recounted, who said Grant "was popularly supposed to move about with sealed lips." This gave the new commander a reputation as the "American Sphinx," "Ulysses the Silent," and "the Great Unspeakable"—all of which harkened back to the early war impression he made as "the quiet man."

**Secretary of War Edwin Stanton suggested *The Council of War* was "one of the most interesting and appropriate occasions" for a sculpture—ironic because the three men held few such conferences. Lincoln preferred to let Grant keep his own council in the field, and Grant communicated with the president and secretary of war remotely. Artist John Rogers created the work circa 1873. Widely reproduced, the original is now housed in the Smithsonian American Art Museum. (cm)**

"It is true that he had no 'small talk' introduced merely for the sake of talking," Porter conceded, "and many a one will recollect the embarrassment of a first encounter with him from this fact. . . ." Years later, writer Mark Twain would recount just such a first meeting during Grant's presidency. After shaking hands, Twain said,

*He did not say a word, but just stood. . . . I could not think of anything to say. . . . There was an awkward pause, a dreary pause, a horrible pause. Then I thought of something, and looked up into the unyielding face, and said timidly, 'Mr. President, I–I am embarrassed. Are you?'*

Grant's face broke—"just a little—a wee glimmer, the momentary flicker of a summer-lightening smile"—and Twain was out the door in a flash. Years later, they would form an enduring friendship.

\*   \*   \*

Grant spent his first month and a half as general in chief in a wild flurry of activity, planning for the spring campaigns. "The resources of the enemy and his numerical strength were far inferior to ours," Grant wrote, and so he determined:

*first, to use the greatest number of troops practicable against the armed force of the enemy, preventing him from using the same force at different seasons against first one and then another of our armies, and eliminating the possibility of repose for refitting and producing necessary supplies for carrying on resistance; second, to hammer continuously against the armed forces of the enemy and his resources, until by mere attrition, if in no other way, there should be nothing left of him. . . .*

With the election on the November horizon, Grant hoped for a "war of annihilation"—an overwhelming military victory that would destroy a Confederate army in one fell swoop that would, ideally, fall as soon as possible. Failing that, Grant counted on a "war of attrition," where math strongly favored the Union effort in terms of men, money, and material. Grant had more of everything and intended to use it all in an effort to wear down and wipe out the Rebellion.

As promised, Grant made his headquarters with the Army of the Potomac, but also as promised, he was as hands-off with Meade's army as Lincoln was with Grant—at least at first. Grant did not know the command staff of Meade's army and did not know who could do what and who could not, so left such operational issues to Meade. Instead, Grant's main directive was strategic. "Lee's army will be your objective point," he instructed on April 9, 1864. "Wherever Lee goes, there you will go also." No one knew it at the time, of course, but it would take exactly one year from the issuance of that order to bring Lee to bay.

Grant then restructured the Army of the Potomac's cavalry. He brought former staff officer James Wilson in to command a division, and he put Phil Sheridan from the Army of the Cumberland in overall cavalry command. Neither man had cavalry experience, but Grant thought both capable officers. He also brought Maj. Gen. Ambrose Burnside and his IX Corps to bolster the army, although issues of rank were prickly and complicated matters for several weeks.

While Meade moved the Army of the Potomac, Grant intended for Sherman to move against Braxton Bragg's replacement. "Neither Atlanta, nor Augusta, nor Savannah, was the objective, but the 'army of Jos. Johnston,' go where it might," Sherman recounted.

Elsewhere, Nathaniel Banks was to extricate himself from his campaign in Louisiana along the Red River in preparation for Grant's long-envisioned move on Mobile. Maj. Gen. Franz Sigel was to move southward up the Shenandoah Valley, which was Virginia's breadbasket and the main source of recruits for Lee's dwindling army. Maj. Gen. George Crook was to disrupt Confederate saltworks in southwest Virginia and sever the rail connection between that area and Tennessee. Finally, Maj. Gen. Benjamin Butler would move up the James Peninsula to approach Richmond from the south.

By moving all forces simultaneously, Grant planned to tie down Confederate forces, preventing them from shifting from theater to theater as reinforcements. It was one more way for the Union to exploit its numerical superiorities.

For all the grand strategy and the high expectations and the confidence of the president, the men of the Army of the Potomac adopted a wait-and-see attitude about this new commander from the West. "There is no enthusiasm in the army for Gen. Grant; and, on the other hand, there is no prejudice against him," said an officer in the 19th Maine Infantry. "We are prepared to throw up our hats for him when he shows himself the great soldier here in Virginia against Lee and the best troops of the rebels."

\*     \*     \*

Lee, on the far side of the Rapidan River, watched and waited. He assumed Grant would launch another "On to Richmond!" campaign of the type his Army of Northern Virginia had already beaten back repeatedly, yet he could do nothing until Grant made the first move. Once Grant did, Lee wanted to pounce. "We must destroy this army of Grant's before he gets to the James River," he told a subordinate. "If he gets there, it will become a siege, and then it will be a mere question of time."

Lee did not know Grant at all, and so this man from the West posed a mystery to him. However, Lee's second in command, James Longstreet, knew Grant well. They had met at West Point and had served together in the "old army" before fighting in the Mexican War. They had been such close friends that Longstreet had attended Grant's 1848 wedding to Julia in St. Louis. "I believe I know him through and through; and I tell you we cannot afford to underrate him and the army he now commands," Longstreet warned. "We must make up our minds to get into line of battle and to stay there; for that man will fight us every day and every hour till the end of the war."

The Army of the Potomac shook itself to life, put out the cook fires, and rumbled out of its camps on May 4, 1864. On the south bank of the Rapidan, Grant stopped to watch the army cross. "A sun as bright as the 'sun of Austerlitz' shone down upon the scene," recalled Horace Porter. "Its light brought out

"[Robert E. Lee] was a good man, a fair commander, who had everything in his favor," Grant wrote. "He was a man who needed sunshine. He was supported by the unanimous voice of the South. . . . Everything he did was right. He was treated like a demi-god." (loc)

in vivid colors the beauties of the landscape which lay before us" and "reflected with dazzling brilliancy from the brass field-pieces and the white covers of the wagons as they rolled lazily in the distance."

Sitting atop his favorite horse, a bay named Cincinnati, Grant looked dressier than usual with a pair of yellowish-brown thread gloves and plain top-boots, reaching to his knees. He even wore a regulation sword, spurs, and sash—highly unusual for him while on campaign—and his black felt slouch hat had a plain gold cord around it.

A reporter caught the general's attention. "General Grant, about how long will it take you to get to Richmond?"

"I will agree to be there in about four days," Grant replied—"that is, if General Lee becomes a party to the agreement; but if he objects, the trip will undoubtedly be prolonged."

Despite the levity, the scene held a dark omen, too, at least for some. Congressman Elihu Washburne, Grant's patron, sat his horse next to Grant. "His plain black, funeral-looking citizen's clothes presented a sight not often witnessed on a general's staff," Porter noted. Soldiers, as they marched past, began "to make audible side remarks": Had Grant brought his private undertaker with him? A parson to read the funeral service over the Confederacy when the boy put it in the "last ditch"?

Grant intended to press matters that far, in any event. As he told another correspondent, "There will be no turning back."

*    *    *

"While the most critical movements were taking place, General Grant manifested no perceptible anxiety, but gave his orders, and sent and received communications, with a coolness and deliberation which made a marked impression upon those who had been brought into contact with him for the first time on the field of battle," wrote Horace Porter. (loc)

"The Ball" opened on the morning of May 5 as the army crossed through a second-growth forest known as "the Wilderness." Truly wild, travelers called it "one of the waste places of nature," choked with thick, dense foliage, heavily forested rolling hills, and swampy lowlands. "A worse place for a battlefield could not be conceived," one Federal officer said.

Grant didn't think Lee would attack him in the Wilderness, the physical limitations of the area being as bad for Lee as for him. Lee felt differently, thinking the terrain's restrictions would make up for his lesser numbers. His army pounced, and Grant—eager for Lee to give him battle whenever and wherever he might—readily accepted the challenge. "If an opportunity presents itself for pitching into a part of Lee's army, do so without giving time for dispositions," he had told Meade.

Grant settled in for news from the front. To pass the time, observed Porter, "He was seated upon the ground with his back against a tree . . . whittling pine sticks." His work with the knife played "sad havoc with the thread gloves," which soon had holes in their fingertips, and so he abandoned them. He also smoked cigars relentlessly, "All very strong and of formidable size." By day's end, he had smoked 20 cigars, which ever after became part of Grant lore, although as Porter asserted, "He never afterward equaled that record in the use of tobacco."

The fight in the Wilderness proved more brutal than anything Grant had yet overseen in the war, outpacing even Shiloh in terms of casualties. Fighting see-sawed over two days along two fronts. On the evening of the second day of battle, Lee launched a flank attack on the end of the battlefield closest to Grant's headquarters. "In the darkness of the night, in the gloom of a tangled forest, and after men's nerves had been racked by the strain of a two days' desperate battle, the most immovable commander might have been shaken," allowed Porter. But witnesses said Grant "showed no emotion whatever in that momentous emergency, but received the news . . . with Spartan calmness and equanimity."

But even Grant's patience had its limits. A frazzled staff officer from the Army of the Potomac bolted into camp, warning of Lee's aggressiveness and

Grant said James Longstreet "was brave, honest, intelligent, a very capable soldier, subordinate to his superiors, just and kind to his subordinates, but jealous of his own rights, which he had the courage to maintain." Longstreet's accidental wounding by his own men in the Wilderness removed the one person in the Army of Northern Virginia who had the most insight into Grant, who was otherwise a stranger to Lee and his commanders. (loc)

The sun, said Porter, "brought out in vivid colors the beauties of the landscape which lay before us, and its rays were reflected with dazzling brilliancy from the brass field-pieces and the white covers of the wagons as they rolled lazily along in the distance. The crisp, bracing air seemed to impart to all a sense of exhilaration. As far as the eye could reach the troops were wending their way to the front. Their war banners, bullet-riddled and battle-stained, floated proudly in the morning breeze." (cwg)

The knoll on which Grant made his headquarters during the battle of the Wilderness is now a stop on the battlefield's driving tour. Part of the ground was saved by the Central Virginia Battlefields Trust. (cm)

prowess and the danger they were all in as a result. Grant took the cigar from his mouth and "with a degree of animation he seldom manifested," replied:

*Oh, I am heartily tired of hearing about what Lee is going to do. Some of you always seem to think he is suddenly going to turn a double somersault, and land in our rear and on both of our flanks at the same time. Go back to your command, and try to think what we are going to do ourselves, instead of what Lee is going to do.*

The Federal line stabilized, and quiet eventually settled over the battlefield, broken by the cries of the wounded lost in the forest and the distant crackle of fires burning through the woods. With calm restored at his headquarters, the immensity of the battle—and his own role as commanding general—settled on Grant's shoulders. According to cavalryman James Wilson, who came into camp around that time,

According to Horace Porter, Grant "would pick up one small twig after another, and sometimes holding the small end away from him would rapidly shave it down to a point; at other times he would turn the point toward him and work on it as if sharpening a lead pencil; then he would girdle it, cut it in two, throw it away, and begin on another." (loc)

*Grant went into his tent, and, throwing himself face downward on his cot, gave way to the greatest emotion, but without uttering any word of doubt or discouragement. What was in his heart can only be inferred, but . . . nothing can be more certain than that he was stirred to the very depths of his soul.*

"No one knew better than he that he was face to face with destiny," Wilson surmised, "and there was no doubt . . . that he realized it fully and understood perfectly that retreat from that field meant a great calamity to his country as well as to himself."

Grant later came out from his tent and sat by the fire, consumed in quiet. He had confronted his own "dark night of the soul" and had come through the fire. No one realized it yet, but it was the turning point of the war.

# The Overland Campaign and Beyond

## CHAPTER TWELVE
### *May 1864–January 1865*

On the evening of May 7, through thick smoke hanging in the air, Grant rode with his staff to an intersection in the woods where the Brock Road and Plank Road came together. Control of the intersection meant control of the battlefield, and so the worst of the fighting had concentrated in that area. Federal earthworks had even caught fire during the climax of a Confederate assault on May 6.

To take the Plank Road eastward meant a retreat to Fredericksburg or the safety of the far side of the Rapidan River. Instead, Grant briefly conferred with some officers at the intersection, reined to his right, and steered his mount down the south-bound Brock Road, which would take the army around Lee's right flank and deeper into Confederate territory. Like a flash, word "passed rapidly along that the chief who had led them through the mazes of the Wilderness was again moving forward with his horse's head turned toward Richmond," Porter recalled:

*Soldiers weary and sleep after their long battle, with stiffened limbs and smarting wounds, now sprang to their feet, forgetful of their pains, and rushed forward to the roadside. Wild cheers echoed*

While Grant did not leave Spotsylvania cowed by Lee, he did have a greater respect for his Confederate counterpart after learning some tough lessons during the first three weeks of the Overland Campaign. (cm)

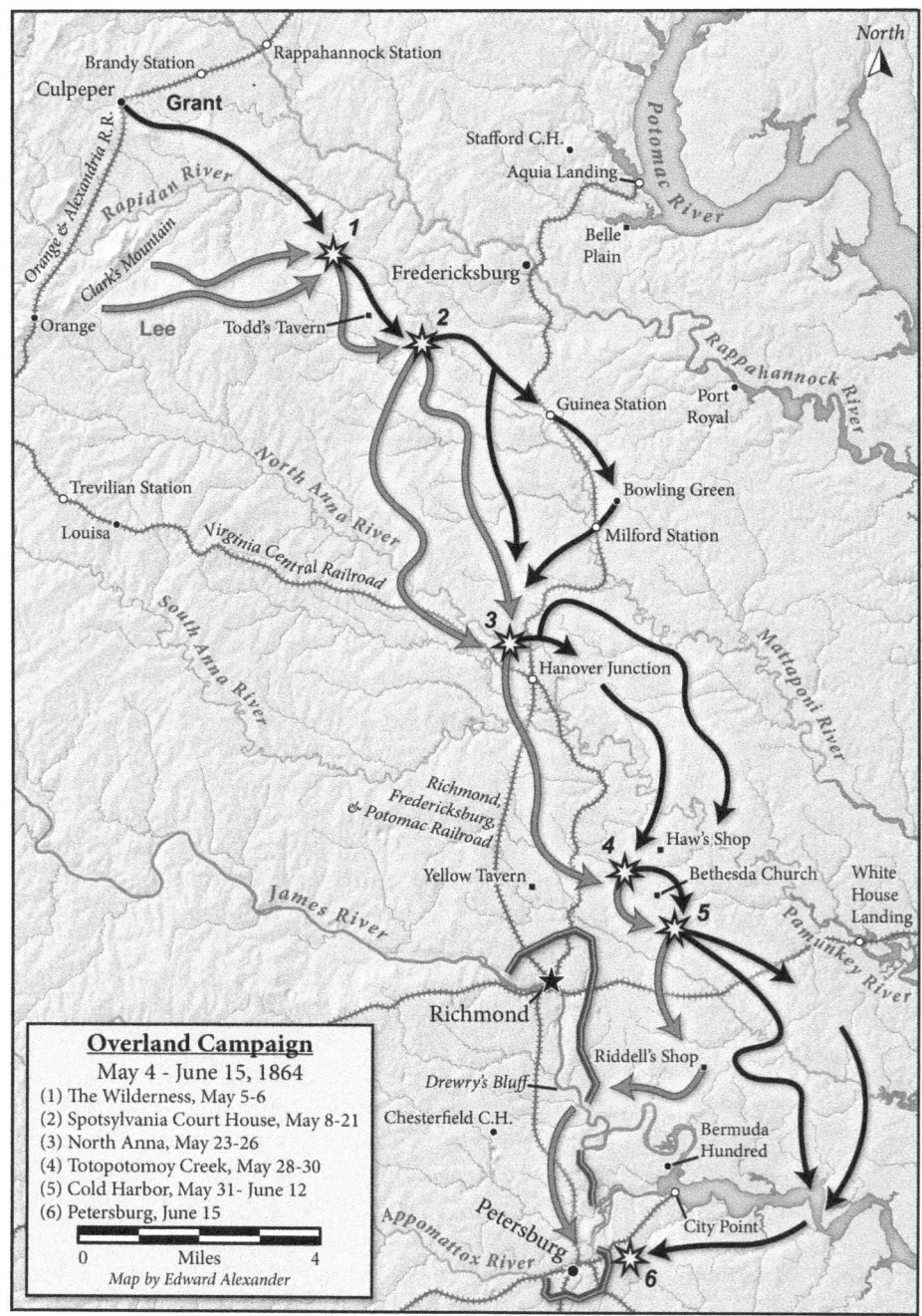

**OVERLAND CAMPAIGN, MAY 4–JUNE 15, 1864**—In the Wilderness, Grant changed the very nature of the war when he chose to forge onward rather than withdraw. The result was a six-week campaign of constant fighting and maneuvering. Lee relied on strong defenses to force tactical draws, but strategically, Grant crept closer to Richmond as he successfully waged his war of attrition.

*through the forest, and glad shouts of triumph rent the air. Men swung their hats, tossed up their arms, and pressed forward to within touch of their chief, clapping their hands, and speaking to him with the familiarity of comrades.*

"The demonstration," Porter said, "was the emphatic verdict pronounced by the troops upon his first battle in the East."

Amidst the cheers, Grant kept a practical mind. "The sound will reach the ears of the enemy," he said, "and I fear it may reveal our movement." Indeed, Confederates—just a few hundred yards away through the dark, close woods—did heard the ruckus, but they thought it meant the Federals were retreating.

Grant had vowed there would be no turning back, but it wasn't so until he actually executed. His grand strategy would have been for naught had he folded under the unprecedented pressure of the battle. He had resolved, the night before, to carry on, and on the morning of May 7, he gave the orders for the move, changing the very nature of how the war would be fought from then on.

The battle of the Wilderness opened a six-week contest that moved, step by step, closer to Richmond. The fighting shifted like a slow-motion tornado from Spotsylvania Court House to the North Anna River to Totopotomoy Creek, and finally to Cold Harbor.

**Although ordered to remain quiet, Federal soldiers at the Brock Road/Plank Road intersection roared their approval when they realized Grant was directing them onward. There would be "no turning back." (loc)**

GRANT TURNING LEE'S FLANK.

**Grant kept moving around Lee's right— "turning the flank."** (loc)

**Historical markers dot the route of the armies from Spotsylvania to Cold Harbor, such as this one on the banks of the North Anna River. Because they were installed in Virginia *by* Virginia, note which general gets top billing.** (cm)

Grant gritted his teeth, kept his stoney resolve, and told Washington, "I intend fight it out along this line if it takes all summer."

Doing so, however, resulted in massive casualties, though: more than 17,000 in the Wilderness (May 5-7); nearly 19,000 at Spotsy (May 8–21); a mere 2,600 at North Anna (May 23–26); nearly 13,000 at Cold Harbor (May 31–June 12). Over the same ground and time, Lee's army lost 30,000 men, totaling a higher percentage of his army. Grant could replace his losses; Lee could not—something that vexed him terribly. "[Grant's] talent and strategy consists in accumulating overwhelming numbers," Lee lamented. Harried as Lee was by the arithmetic in Grant's favor, his assessment overlooked Grant's tenacity, his willingness to maneuver, and his ability to improvise and adapt.

It was during this campaign that the phrase "Grant the Butcher" first appeared—an insult that has been used by Grant critics ever since. According to this portrayal of Grant, he racked up high casualties through mindless, uncreative frontal assaults, and only his superior numbers achieved victory despite all the bloodshed—bloodshed that critics felt Grant didn't care about. This contrived stereotype achieved widespread acceptance because of the postwar propaganda efforts of the "Lost Cause," which tried to justify Confederate defeat by undermining Federal victory, and Grant because its key casualty.

However, the phrase actually made its debut on May 11, 1864, in a *northern* newspaper. The *Washington* (PA) *Reporter* quoted a Copperhead— an anti-war Democrat—who hoped "the butcher Grant can be snubbed in the South."

The cost of battle was never far from Grant's mind, though. "[H]e was visibly affected by his proximity to the wounded, and especially by the sight of blood," Porter said. "He would turn his face away from such scenes, and show by the expression of his countenance, and sometimes by a pause in his conversation, that he felt most keenly the painful spectacle presented by the field of battle." When someone asked Grant about it, he said, "I cannot bear the sight of suffering."

Porter recounted a similar episode from May 18 at Spotsylvania, where Grant and his staff passed a group of wounded men alongside the road. "[O]ne of them, who was lying close to the roadside, seemed to attract his special notice . . ." Porter wrote. "The blood was flowing from a wound in his breast, the froth about his mouth was tinged with red, and his wandering, staring eyes gave unmistakable evidence of approaching death." At that moment, a young officer bolted past on his horse, splashing mud on the dying man's face. "He gave a piteous look . . ." Porter noticed. "The general, whose eyes were at that moment turned upon the youth, was visibly affected." Grant reined in his horse to dismount, but Porter hopped down to tend the soldier, but the man died within moments.

On the way out of Spotsylvania, Grant's guide lost his way for a short time. "General Grant at first demurred when it was proposed to turn back, and urged the guide to try and find some cross-road leading to the Brock road, to avoid retracing our steps," recounted Horace Porter. "This was an instance of his marked aversion to turning back, which amounted almost to a superstition. He often put himself to the greatest personal inconvenience to avoid it. When he found he was not traveling in the direction he intended to take, he would try all sorts of cross-cuts, ford streams, and jump any number of fences to reach another road rather than go back and take a fresh start." (cwg)

"There was a painfully sad look upon the general's face, and he did not speak for some time," Porter recalled. "While always keenly sensitive to the sufferings of the wounded, this pitiful sight seemed to affect him more than usual."

*   *   *

How ironic critics would have found it that "Grant the Butcher" liked his meat "cooked almost to a crisp." "[T]he nearer [the cook] came to burning up the beef the better the general liked it," Porter later noted, adding later, "If blood appeared in any meat which came on the table, the sight of it seemed entirely to destroy his appetite." (ac/cm)

As the campaign unfolded, Grant's hands-off approach with the Army of the Potomac became more hands on. "[A]t first I had maneuvered the army," Meade wrote, "but that gradually, and from the very nature of things, Grant had taken control." Meade recognized "it would be injurious to the army to have two heads" and so submitted to his secondary role. "If there was any honorable way of retiring from my present false position, I would undoubtedly adopt it," he told his wife just before the armies left Spotsylvania, "but there is none and all I can do is patiently submit and bear with resignation the humiliation." Meade tried to give Grant the benefit of the doubt. "[I]t is idle to deny that my position is a very unjust one," he admitted, but "I believe it is not intentional on his part, but arises from the force of circumstances."

While Grant eventually became "embarrassed" by Meade's position, he forged onward much as he did through the campaign itself. The two would never become friends the way Grant and Sherman had, but Grant knew he could count on Meade's professionalism. "Meade's loyalty and soldierly qualities were so high, that, whether he approved or disapproved a movement, he made no difficulty about the performance of his duty," Grant later said.

In fact, on May 13, Grant put Meade forward for promotion. "General Meade has more than met my sanguine expectations," he wrote in a dispatch to Washington. "He and Sherman are the fittest officers for large commanders I have come in contact with. If their services can be rewarded to

the ranks of major-generals in the regular army the honor would be worthily bestowed, and I would feel personally gratified. I would not like to see one of these promotions at the time without seeing both." Considering Grant's closeness with Sherman, such an endorsement says volumes about Meade. Meade's promotion would run into complications in Washington for a variety of reasons, and it would take months for Grant to push it through, although Sherman's sailed through smoothly.

Meade knew he wasn't the favorite, and he received a reminder on May 24. The commanders and their staffs made their headquarters together at Carmel Church, just north of the North Anna River. Staffers laid boards across the pews to make a table for Grant and Meade to work. "Pretty soon we had a fine blow-up!" recalled Theodore Lyman, a volunteer aide on Meade's staff.

*Grant leans over Meade's shoulders during a break at Massaponax Church on the way out of Spotsylvania. No image could better capture the working relationship between the two, which proved tense for Meade, especially.* (loc)

A coded message arrived from Sherman, which the "gossipy" Charles Dana read aloud. The army in the west had fought and maneuvered, it said, and "if Grant could inspire the Potomac army to do a proper degree of fighting, the success could not be doubted." On the heels of the Wilderness and Spotsylvania, such a dispatch was too much for Meade.

"Sir! I consider that dispatch an insult to the army I command, and to me personally," Meade snapped, his eyes "like a rattlesnake's" rather than like those of a goggle-eyed snapping turtle from which he got his nickname. "The Army of the Potomac does not require General Grant's inspiration or anybody else inspiration to make it fight!"

The next couple of weeks were probably the tensest of their relationship, moreso on Meade's part than on his commander's. As Grant took more operational control, Meade became more peevish and

**General Meade's "irritability of temper, and over sensitiveness to implied censure or criticism" led him in mid-July to tender his resignation in a pique of anger. Grant soothed his feelings and talked him out of it. In general, they consulted frequently.** (ac/cm)

showed less initiative: if Grant was going to call the shots, then by all means, Meade would let him. A chill would develop that would lead to disjointed attacks at Cold Harbor and a couple of weeks later at the gates of Petersburg.

"I have always regretted that the last assault at Cold Harbor was ever made . . ." Grant would famously write. "[N]o advantage whatever was gained to compensate for the heavy loss we sustained."

Following that ill-fated attack, dead and wounded men littered the field. Without a truce, no one could venture out to help them, but Grant and Lee could not settle on terms for doing so. Instead, they spent days dickering over army protocol as wounded men suffered from their injuries and from thirst, and many of them expired. To call for a truce, though, was to blink—something neither man felt he could afford to do because of its impact on public perception.

\*    \*    \*

One of the most iconic photos of Grant was taken at Cold Harbor on June 11 or 12, 1864. (loc)

From Cold Harbor, men in the trenches could see the steeples of Richmond's churches just a few miles distant. Lee still blocked the way, but backed up as he was against the city, he had also lost his ability to maneuver. The Army of the Potomac, meanwhile, was now close enough to unite with Benjamin Butler's Army of the James, which Confederates had bottled up along the James River.

Grant sent the Army of the Potomac south of the James to Petersburg in an attempt to outflank Lee again. Lee was slow to counter, but poor coordination between Meade and Butler's forces—led on the expedition by the once-slighted "Baldy" Smith—prevented a Federal breakthrough. Instead of securing a decisive battlefield victory against the vital rail center, Grant had to settle into siege operations.

Lee had dreaded this, because he knew time worked against the Confederacy because of its dwindling resources. However, if the Confederates could just hold on until the November election, Northern discontent might be bad enough to oust

Lincoln from office. So, in the short term, at least, time became a Confederate ally.

Grant knew this and kept operations as active as possible, extending the Federal position in an attempt to outflank Confederates. He launched attacks whenever possible. None reached the scope and scale of the opening battle for Petersburg June 15–18 or the battles of the Overland Campaign. One of them, a botched attempt to blow up a mine beneath Confederates lines—later known as the battle of the Crater—did manage the dubious distinction as one of the war's great disasters. "It was the saddest affair I have witnessed in this war," Grant wrote to Halleck. He later characterized it as "a stupendous failure."

At the end of September, Grant came under fire at the front. Federals launched an attack that captured a Confederate position called Fort Harrison, and after, Grant went to see the position for himself. The ground, reported Porter, was "so torn with shot and shell and covered with killed and wounded in some places that the general had to pick his way in stepping over the dead bodies that lay in his path. He turned his looks upward to avoid as much as possible, the ghastly sight, and the expression of profound grief impressed upon his future told, as usual, the effect produced upon him by the sad spectacle."

At the edge of the works, Grant could distinctly see the church spires of Petersburg, as well as the Confederate fallback position. He stepped back into the ruins of the fort and sat, cross-legged, to write out plans for a continued attack. Confederates, meanwhile, began to lob shells at the fort, still hoping to dislodge the Federals from their newly won position. One of those shells burst directly over Grant's head. "[T]hose standing about instinctively

**Grant was under fire— literally—at Fort Harrison when a shell burst over his head.** (cwg)

ducked their heads, but he paid no attention to the occurrence, and did not pause in his writing, or even look up," Porter noted. No one was injured.

Grant did not succeed in breaking the deadlock with Lee on that occasion, but Federals had met with success elsewhere. On September 2, Sherman had finally captured Atlanta, news that "set the country all aglow," Grant said. "This was the first great political campaign for the Republicans and their canvas of 1864." Then, Maj. Gen. Phil Sheridan, under Grant's orders, secured a "decisive victory" in the Shenandoah Valley, which Grant characterized as "the most effective campaign argument" for Lincoln up to that point. "[T]hese two campaigns probably had more effect in settling the election of the following November than all the speeches, all the bonfires, and all the parading with banners and bands of music in the north." As the architect of the Union's grand strategy, Grant could rightfully take credit for these successes.

*    *    *

During Grant's time at Petersburg, he made his headquarters at City Point, at the junction of the James and Appomattox Rivers. His camp sat atop a high bluff that overlooked the bay-like expanse of water created by the wide rivers. "There was a nest of scattered houses here, with a church or two . . ." wrote Meade staffer Theodore Lyman. "Near a once-pretty cottage, just on the point, Grant had pitched his tents."

A wharf at the base of the bluffs made a convenient landing for transports, although the area would soon expand into one of the busiest inland ports in the country. Ships could sail from the Chesapeake, up the James, to bring supplies for Grant's armies. Warehouses sprang up. So did a 600-patient hospital, which Grant visited frequently. Telegraph lines snaked out to various command posts along the front, and crews even strung a line—which needed constant maintenance—across Hampton roads to Fort Monroe, providing direct access to Washington.

The commander of the garrison, in an effort to show hospitality, organized a brass band to serenade

**Grant's headquarters at City Point is now managed as a unit of Petersburg National Military Park.** (cm)

Grant nightly. By the third evening, Grant had heard enough and asked Porter to ask them to "cease firing." "I fear that band-master's feelings have been hurt," Grant admitted, "but I didn't want him to be wasting his time upon a person who has no ear for music." Indeed, Grant's tin ear was notorious. "I know only two tunes. One of them is 'Yankee Doodle'—and the other isn't," he is commonly misquoted as saying. In truth, the second song was the spiritual hymn "Old One Hundred," a.k.a., "The Doxology." (Years later, after being constantly serenaded by "Hail to the Chief" during his presidency, Grant would joke that he added a third tune to his musical repertoire.)

When Lincoln paid a visit to City Point in June, everything about his experience with Grant impressed him. "When Grant once gets possession of a place, he holds onto it as if he had inherited it," the president observed. He encouraged Grant to keep doing what he had been doing, despite the casualties that had accumulated and the sagging Northern morale that went with them—an indirect reminder to Grant about the importance of the election.

"I saw a great deal of [the president] at City point," Grant recalled later, "for he seemed glad to get away from the cares and anxieties of the capital."

An entire stream of dignitaries visited at various times: Secretary of State William Seward, Secretary of War Edwin Stanton, Army of the Cumberland commander George Thomas, and Grant's friend Sherman.

In August, Grant's most anticipated visitors arrived: Julia and the children. They stayed on their steamer, tied up at the wharf, since no appropriate quarters existed for them at camp. Julia had visited her husband on several occasions in the west, though, and "had learned perfectly how to adapt herself to camp life." She got along well with the staff and, like her husband, visited the hospital to encourage the sick and wounded.

She quickly became a great favorite at the hospital and among the soldiers throughout camp.

The August trip was short, but the quartermaster's department undertook the job of repairing the rundown cottage atop the bluff so the Grants would have a proper place to stay. In December, Julia returned for an extended visit.

Trusting her implicitly, Grant conducted business as usual in her presence, discussing plans and strategies. During a winter visit from William T. Sherman, as the two generals discussed Sherman's plans for what became his Carolina campaign, Grant suddenly looked at his wife, sitting across the room. "Sherman," he asked, "do you think it is safe to let Mrs. Grant hear us?"

"Well, I don't know," Sherman replied. "Let me see. Mrs. Grant, can you tell me where the Tombigbee River is?"

Julia answered "wide of the mark, of course," as she later recounted the episode.

Sherman then inquired, looking much puzzled himself, "Can you tell me where the Chattahoochee River is? That was what I wanted, not the Tombigbee."

Julia, "throwing dust in Sherman's eyes," admitted she had forgotten where that was, as well.

**This image, circulated around the turn of the century, purported to show "Grant at City Point." In fact, the image was fake. According to the Library of Congress: "Three photos provided different parts of the portrait. The Library has negatives or prints that show (1) the head, from Grant at his Cold Harbor, Va. headquarters; (2) the horse and man's body, from Maj. Gen. Alexander McDowell McCook; and (3) the background, from Confederate prisoners captured in the battle of Fisher's Hill, Va."** (loc)

Sherman turned back to Grant. "Oh, yes, Grant. I think we may trust her."

The exchange gave everyone a good chuckle.

At other times, Grant would joke with Julia by giving her "a fanciful description of an imaginary campaign, in which he would name impossible figures as to the number of the troops, inextricably, confused the geography of the country, and trace out a plan of marvelously complicated movements in a manner that was often exceedingly droll."

Glimpses of the couple in private showed them "as bashful as two young lovers spy upon in the scenes of their courtship." She called him "Ulys" and, in private, by the pet name "Victor." She'd first tried the nickname on for size back in the spring of 1861 when Grant had read to her about "the triumphs of Victor Emmanuel," the general who had united Italy and ascended to its throne in March of that year—although Grant's string of battlefield successes had since given the nickname a more personal meaning.

**A casual Jesse Grant (center) joins his parents at City Point.** (loc)

For their oldest son, Fred, being back with the army in August offered adventure. He had campaigned with his father on the road to Vicksburg, so a new stint in army "service" delighted him. His youngest brother, Jesse, got the opportunity for an extended stay following the Christmas holiday.

Grant enjoyed unique relationships with each of his children, delighting in their "idiosyncrasies," as biographer Ron Chernow described them: "treating sturdy Fred like a young man; exercising care with the smart but delicate Buck; being tender with his beloved Nellie, and rejoicing in the antics of mischievous Jesse."

Porter walked into Grant's tent one day to find the general entangled with the two oldest boys, Fred and Ulysses Jr., known as Buck. Grant "had become red in the face, and seemed nearly out of breath from the exertion," Porter recalled. "The lads had just tripped him up, and he was on his knees on the floor, grappling with the youngsters, and joining in their merry laughter, as if he were a boy again himself."

Disentangling himself from the young combatants, Grant rose to greet his staff officer and attended to the business brought before him. "Ah, you know my weaknesses," Grant said: "my children and my horses."

*    *    *

Twice, danger came to City Point.

The first trouble came on August 9. Grant sat in a camp stool in front of his tent late that morning, surrounded by several staff members, receiving a report about spies in the camp. At 11:40 a.m., "a terrific explosion shook the earth." Then, as Porter recalled, "there rained down upon the party a terrific shower of shells, bullets, boards, and fragments of timber." Most of the staff bolted toward the bluff, although Grant, unhurt, remained in place while they investigated. A boat loaded with ordinance and docked at the wharf at the foot of the hill had exploded, killing 43 people and injuring 40 others. A Confederate spy

"[E]very part of the yard used as my headquarters is filled with splinters and shells," Grant observed after the explosion at the wharf, sketched here by Alfred Waud. (loc)

had smuggled "an infernal machine" on board, set with a timing device that allowed him to slip away before the explosion—although it would be years until anyone would learn the true cause, and only then because the perpetrator admitted it.

The incident drew stark attention to how vulnerable Grant really was, inspiring his staff to set up a secret detail of watchers to function as bodyguards without Grant's knowledge.

The second incident, on January 24, seemed more worrisome at first but ended up being far less so. The James River, running high, made it possible for Confederates to run gunboats past obstructions Federals had placed between City Point and Richmond. Just past 1:00 a.m., a frantic staff officer awoke Grant: "General, the rebel rams are coming down the river and have passed the obstructions!" As Porter explained, "There was an enormous accumulation of supplies at City Point, and their destruction at this time would have been a serious embarrassment." A bombardment would also put the Federal high command at risk.

Grant threw his long boots and uniform coat over his pajamas, lit a cigar, and stomped into his office where he began to write out orders. As at the Wilderness months earlier, "the only expression of excitement was the rapid and sharp puff of his cigars," Julia recounted, saying "it was like a little steam engine."

"Will the gunboats shell the bluff?" Julia asked.

"Yes, of course," Grant replied.

But as it turned out, five of the six gunboats failed to pass the obstructions. The sixth dashed through, but Federal gunners crippled it, leaving it "utterly helpless" just beyond the obstructions, unable to move. The danger to City Point never materialized.

*   *   *

Days after the gunboat incident, on January 29, three Confederate peace commissioners materialized along the lines under flag of truce. Grant met them—"our relations were pleasant, and I found them all very agreeable gentlemen"—and he wired to Washington for instructions. On February 3, Lincoln met the commissioners on a steamboat, the *River Queen*, near Fort Monroe. The Hampton Roads Peace Conference, as it came to be known, ended in failure because Confederates refused to make concessions on independence or emancipation. The outcome satisfied Grant, who said, "There have been too great a waste of blood and treasure to concede anything of the kind."

While we do not know Lincoln's final blueprint for peace, we know he spent considerable time talking over the matter with Sherman, Grant, and Porter, as imagined in this 1868 painting, *The Peacemakers,* by George P. A. Healy. (whha)

Otherwise, action along the Federal lines was generally quiet over the winter. "[T]here was frequent skirmishing between pickets, but no serious battle spot near either Petersburg or Richmond," Grant reported in his memoirs. "It would prolong this work to give a detailed count of all that took place from day to day around Petersburg and other parts of my command, and it would not interest the general reader if given."

**The diminutive Confederate Vice President Alexander Stephens** served as one of the peace commissioners. "I have been a particular admirer of Mr. Stephens," Grant said. "I had always posed that he was a very small

man, but when I saw him in the dusk of the evening, I was very much surprised to find so large man as he seemed to be.... [H]e was wearing a coarse gray woolen overcoat. . . . The overcoat extended nearly into his feet, and was so large that gave him the appearance of being an average-sized man. He took this off when he reached the cabin of the boat, and I was struck with the apparent change in size, in the coat and out of it." Lincoln, who likewise saw Stephens in the coat, called it "the biggest shuck and the littlest ear that you ever did see."

_Appomattox_

# CHAPTER THIRTEEN
## _Spring 1865_

As spring neared, Grant became anxious. "I felt that the situation of the Confederate army was such that they would try to make an escape at the earliest practicable moment, and I was afraid, every morning, that I would wake from my sleep to hear that Lee had gone, and that nothing was left, but a picket line." Winter desertions had emaciated Lee's army, and constant skirmishing had frayed the nerves of the exhausted men who had remained. "[I]t was a question of arithmetic to calculate how long they could hold out . . ." Grant knew.

On March 25, Confederates tried to break through the Federal line at a place called Fort Stedman, but they did not have the strength or discipline to maintain their momentum. Like Grant's men at Belmont years earlier, they found themselves amidst the plenty of the Federal camps and were "demoralized" by their own success. Days later, on April 1, on the far west flank of both lines, Federals secured a victory that inspired Grant to launch an all-out assault against the Confederate line the next morning.

The Federals punched through.

Lee held on as best he could into the night of April 2, but under the cover of darkness and in the

**Appomattox Court House would become a defining place for Grant—and for the nation.** (ac/cf)

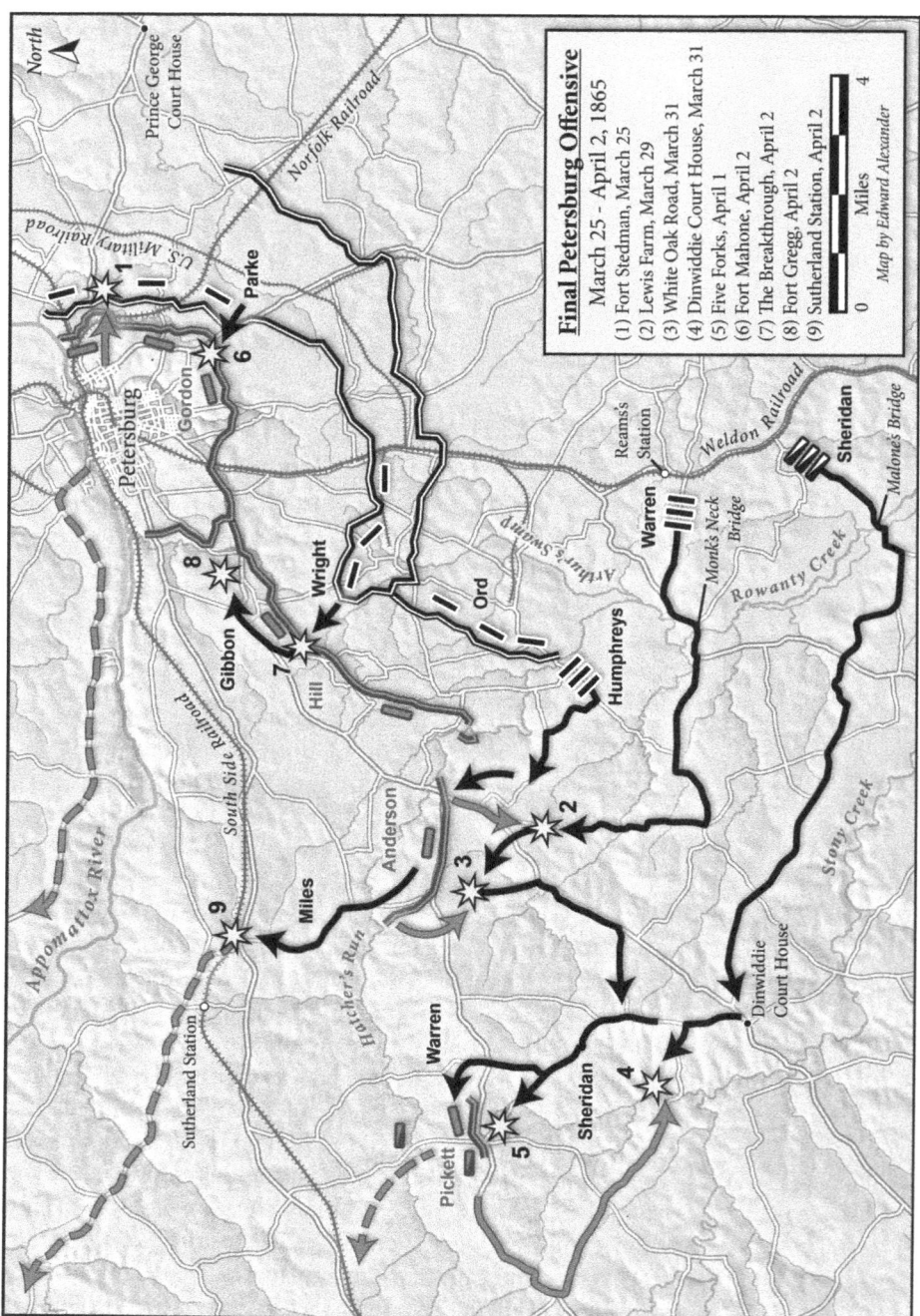

FINAL PETERSBURG OFFENSIVE, MARCH 25–APRIL 2, 1865—The final days of March saw a flurry of activity along the overextended Confederate line, which demonstrated just how weakened Confederate forces were. Grant decided on a major push at dawn on April 2, which proved decisive. Lee had hoped to break out and unite his army with an army commanded by Joseph E. Johnston, but instead had to flee with his men to the west.

face of Federal pressure, he evacuated his army from Petersburg and Richmond and fled west. Grant immediately ordered a pursuit. In their haste to escape, Confederates "threw away caissons, ammunition, clothing, and almost anything to lighten their loads, and pushed up along the Appomattox River . . ." Grant recorded.

Before Grant set out with his army on April 3, he entertained a visit from President Lincoln, who had been waiting at City Point. "We had selected the piazza of a deserted house," Grant wrote of the meeting. Around them, "not a soul to be seen, not even an animal in the streets." Except for Grant's staff and a small cavalry escort, "There was absolutely no one there...."

When Lincoln arrived, he congratulated Grant on his victory and offered his thanks to the army for achieving it. "Do you know, general, that I have had a sort of sneaking idea for some days that you intended to do something like this," Lincoln added.

They chatted for some little while—a conversation that no one overheard, that Grant did not record in detail, and that Lincoln did not live long enough to recount at all. Lincoln mounted his horse and returned to City Point; Grant mounted up and followed his army.

On Lee's westward flight, he sought rations for his men but promised provisions never arrived. He also tried to turn southward in the hope of uniting with the large Confederate army under Joseph E. Johnston in North Carolina. Federal cavalry blocked the road, forcing Lee further west. "It now became

**Grant conferred with Lincoln prior to joining the pursuit of Lee. Lincoln, meanwhile, went with his son, Tad, and Admiral Porter to Richmond to inspect the fallen Confederate capital.** (cwg)

a life and death struggle with Lee to get south to his provisions," Grant recounted.

The armies clashed again at Sailor's Creek on April 6. The Federal victory netted one-quarter of Lee's remaining army—more than 7,700 men, including Lee's oldest son. One of the captives, Lt. Gen. Richard Ewell, passed word to Grant that "he knew their cause was lost . . . that for every man that was killed after this in the war somebody is responsible, and it would be but very little better than murder." Yet he did not think Lee would consent to surrender. Indeed, Lee's survivors continued their flight westward.

Grant wired news of the victory to Lincoln immediately, including an assessment from Sheridan at the front: "If the thing is pressed I think that Lee will surrender."

"Let the thing be pressed," Lincoln replied.

With Federal forces pressing Lee and positioning themselves to encircle his army, Grant sent Lee a letter on April 7. "The results of the last week must convince you of the hopelessness of further resistance on the part of the Army of Northern Virginia in this struggle," he wrote. "I feel that it is so, and regard it as my duty to shift from myself the responsibility of any further effusion of blood, by asking of you of the surrender of . . . the Army of Northern Virginia."

Lee replied that evening. He did not believe the situation was as hopeless as Grant suggested, but likewise wanted to avoid useless bloodshed. "[A]nd therefore before considering your proposition, [I] ask the terms you will offer on condition of its surrender," Lee wrote.

"[P]eace being my great desire," Grant had but one condition, which he shared with Lee the next day: "that the men and officers surrendered shall be disqualified for taking up arms against the Government of the United States until properly exchanged." He offered to meet at a time and place of Lee's choosing to discuss details.

"I did not intend to propose the surrender of the Army of Northern Virginia," Lee responded. But, he added, if a meeting between the two commanders might result in "the restoration of peace, I should be pleased to meet you. . . ."

Even as the written parlay continued, Lee also continued his flight—but by the morning of April 9, Grant's men blocked the path. "The head of Lee's column came marching up there on the morning of the 9th, not dreaming, I suppose, that there were any Union soldiers near," Grant recalled.

"A sharp engagement ensued," he continued, "but Lee quickly set up a white flag."

\*    \*    \*

Grant didn't get Lee's note about peace talks until late on the night of April 8. The unrelenting pace and stress of the pursuit was taking its physical toll on the commander, who was "suffering very severely with a sick headache. . . ." Encamped for the night in an old farmhouse, he spent the night bathing his feet in hot water and mustard and applying mustard plasters on his wrists and on the back of his neck.

When Lee's note finally arrived, it must have felt a little like the runaround. "I have no authority to treat on the subject of peace," Grant wrote in reply. He was anxious for peace with Lee and the Army of Northern Virginia and "the whole North entertains the same feeling," he added. However, the terms for peace were "well understood": "By the South laying down their arms they will hasten that most desirable event, save thousands of human lives, and hundreds of millions of property not yet destroyed."

The migraine lingered into morning and plagued Grant as he rode toward the front. Along the way, an officer reached him with news of the white flag and a reply from Lee: "I now request an interview in accordance with the offer contained in your letter of yesterday."

"[T]he instant I saw the contents of the note I was cured," Grant said of his "sick headache." While some men worried Lee's note was a ruse, Grant "had no doubt about the good faith of Lee."

Soon, the two men found themselves seated together in the parlor of a private home on the edge of the village of Appomattox Courthouse. Caught off guard by Lee's offer to meet, Grant had come straight from the field and "consequently was in rough garb." Compared to Lee, who wore his finest dress uniform,

**Grant and Lee met in the parlor of Wilmer McLean's home. McLean had lived outside Manassas, Virginia, when the war broke out, and part of the first battle of Bull Run was fought on his farm. He later liked to say, "The war began in my front yard and ended in my front parlor."** (loc)

the unadorned Grant wore only a private's blouse and coat, with shoulder straps to indicate his rank. Nor did he have his ceremonial dress sword. "I must have contrasted very strangely with a man so handsomely dressed, six feet high and of faultless form," Grant later realized.

Grant could not get a read on Lee, who "was a man of much dignity, with an impassible face . . .":

> *Whatever his feelings, they were entirely concealed from my observation; but my own feelings, which had been quite jubilant on the receipt of his letter, were sad and depressed. I felt like anything rather than rejoicing at the downfall of a foe who had fought so long and valiantly, and had suffered so much for a cause, though that cause was, I believe, one of the worst for which a people ever fought, and one for which there was the least excuse.*

After small talk about their time in the old army—which Grant remembered as "pleasant"—Lee finally called Grant's attention to the object of their meeting. They discussed terms, which Grant's secretary, Col. Ely Parker, wrote out for both men to sign. Far from the old "unconditional surrender," Grant offered lenient terms in line with Lincoln's desire to "let 'em up easy." Confederates were to stack arms, receive

The chairs from the McLean parlor are now on display in the Smithsonian Institution. (cm)

paroles, and return home until officially exchanged—which, of course, would never happen. Officers could keep their personal horses, sidearms, and baggage. Grant also ordered the distribution of rations to the Confederate soldiers.

"This will have the best possible effect upon the men," Lee admitted. "It will be very gratifying, and will do much toward conciliating our people."

After arranging a few other details, "Lee and I then separated as cordially as we had met." The two men shook hands, then Lee stepped outside and called for his horse. Once mounted, he glanced toward Grant, standing on the front porch. Grant tipped his hat in salute, and Grant's entire staff repeated the gesture. Lee returned it, then rode away.

"General Lee surrendered the Army of Northern Virginia this afternoon on terms proposed by myself," Grant wrote in a telegram to Washington. The news also rippled through the army. Somewhere, an artillery cannonade opened in celebration, but Grant immediately ordered a stop to it. "The Confederates were now our prisoners, and we did not want to exult over their downfall," he later explained.

Grant and Lee met one more time the next morning. Grant rode out toward Lee's headquarters, and when Lee saw him coming, he mounted up and rode out to meet him. "We had there between the lines,

A member of the Tonawanda Seneca, Ely Parker joined Grant's staff as adjutant at the start of the Chattanooga Campaign. He eventually became Grant's military secretary, and he wrote out the surrender terms at Appomattox. Lee, upon being introduced to Parker, extended his hand and said, "I am glad to see one real American here." Parker shook the offered hand and replied, "We are all Americans." (loc)

**Grant wrote to Washington, D.C., at once with the news to Lee's surrender.** (nps)

sitting on horseback, a very pleasant conversation of over half an hour," Grant recounted. Grant encouraged Lee to try and persuade the Confederate government to follow his example and lay down arms everywhere, but Lee seemed noncommittal. "I knew there was no use to urge him to do anything against his idea of what was right," Grant concluded.

Grant also returned to the McLean house, where he caught up with his old friends James Longstreet and Cadmus Wilcox, both of whom had served with Grant in the prewar army and had stood up for him at his wedding to Julia. Grant shook hands and offered cigars. "Pete, let us have another game of brag [a card

"[T]here was an apple orchard on the side of the hill occupied by Confederate forces . . ." Grant recounted in his memoir. "General Babcock, of my staff, reported to me that when he first met General Lee he was sitting upon this embankment with his feet in the road below and his back resting against the tree. The story had no other foundation than that." Yet that story took on a life of its own, and somehow word spread through the Union army that Grant himself had met Lee under the tree. Souvenir hunters soon appeared and chopped the tree up, roots and all. "Like many other stories, it would be very good if it was only true," Grant said. (loc)

game], to recall the old days that were so pleasant to us all," Grant offered.

"Great God . . ." Longstreet thought afterward, "how my heart swells out to such a magnanimous touch of humanity! Why do men fight who were born to be brothers?"

Confederate General John Brown Gordon, who met Grant then for the first time, was deeply impressed by Grant's "modest demeanor." As he later wrote, "There was nothing in the expression of his face or in his language or general bearing which indicated exultation at the great victory he had won."

The Federal commander stayed in Appomattox only another hour or so before Grant and his staff and a small escort struck out for the railroad. He was anxious to get back to Washington. There was much work yet to be done, and a war still underway.

\*　　\*　　\*

It would take another two months for Confederate armies elsewhere to lay down their arms; the last would be Brig. Gen. Stand Watie in Oklahoma in mid-June. By then, a new president, Andrew Johnson, would be overseeing the reconstruction of Southern states and the process of readmitting them to the Union. Grant would come to describe it as a tumultuous time of "foolishness of the President and the blindness of the Southern people to their own interest."

President Lincoln had lived long enough to see the fall of Richmond and the Confederate government

and hear news of Lee's surrender. On April 13, he saw Grant when the general returned to Washington. The president asked Grant to escort the First Lady on a carriage ride around the lavishly lit-up city, where exultant crowds celebrated Lee's surrender. "The people were wild with enthusiasm," observed Horace Porter, and they greeted Grant with "every possible demonstration of delight."

When Grant first arrived in the capital, he had immediately thrown himself into the mountain of paperwork necessary to direct war efforts in the theaters still active, but by the next day, April 14, he was "pretty well through with this work," he said, "and so able to visit my children, who were then in Burlington, New Jersey." Grant and Julia determined that day to set out northward.

In doing so, they had to decline an offer from the president to attend a production that evening at Ford's Theater. And so it was that the Grants were in Philadelphia when a concerned party intercepted their travel with news of Lincoln's assassination.

"It would be impossible for me to describe the feeling that overcame me at the news . . ." Grant wrote,

What if it had been Ulysses and Julia Grant in the presidential box at Ford's Theatre with President and Mrs. Lincoln instead of Maj. Henry Rathbone and his fianceé? (loc)

twenty years later. "I knew of his goodness of heart, his generosity, his yielding disposition, his desire to have everybody happy, and above all his desire to see all the people of the United States enter again upon the full privileges of citizenship with equality among all."

Grant escorted Julia the rest of the way to Burlington, just an hour away, then immediately returned to Washington. All the while—and for the rest of his life—he would be haunted by the thought that, perhaps, things might have turned out differently had he accepted Lincoln's invitation to the theater.

# Epilogue

## July 1885

On July 20, 1885, Ulysses S. Grant "put aside his pencil and said there was nothing more to do."

So recounted his publisher, Mark Twain. The book that had kept Grant alive was done: 1,231 pages across two volumes, totaling 291,000 words, written over 11 months.

It turned out "the quiet man," the man who "maintained an imperturbable silence" and kept his own counsel, who let other people make speeches on his behalf—who sat silently in the rain at Shiloh and who whittled in silence in the Wilderness—it turned out that man had something to say. He had not only helped save the country and helped it achieve its "new birth of freedom," he had lived a remarkable personal story. He worked his way from obscurity in April 1861 to being a colonel by mid-June to being a brigadier general just seven weeks after that. Less than three years later, he commanded every single soldier wearing a blue uniform anywhere in the country. It had been a dizzying, meteoric ascent.

He was keenly aware of his good fortune. He thought often of the hundreds of thousands of men who never made it home from the war—as many as 750,000 by some modern estimates. And each of

Grant's illness was national news. On the porch at Mt. McGregor, he had the surreal experience of reading the newspapers to follow his own medical progress. (ac/cf)

**Grant (to the left by the post) leans out for a better view during the Grand Review of the Armies on May 23–24, 1865. A celebration of the United States' victory in the war, the event also represented the fractured and contentious new world order under President Andrew Johnson (visible, blurry just above Grant).** (loc)

those lost men left behind a broken family, a wife, a child, a parent whose lives were ever-after shattered. And beyond the dead were the men who went home with wounds, physical and emotional, expected to somehow pick back up where they had left off and carry on with life.

It was, Grant said with understatement, "a very bloody and very costly war."

And yet so much remained unwritten. He didn't write about his presidency or offer an account of Reconstruction. He didn't write about his two-year trip around the world, feted by all the heads of state. He didn't write about the business partner who had swindled and bankrupted his family—the incident that triggered the writing project in the first place.

He just didn't have time.

There were even parts of the war he didn't address fully. By the time he got to the Overland Campaign, for instance, he keenly felt the agony in his throat and the narcotic effects of his pain killers. "I should change Spotts if I was able, and could improve N. Anna and Cold Harbor," he told his son Fred, working as a fact-checker, in early July. But he *wasn't* able—not with the manuscript unfinished. He saw its inadequacies, understood its flaws. "If I could have two weeks of strength I could improve it very much," he admitted to Twain at the end of June.

There were also parts of the war he left out on purpose. He avoided discussion of his puzzling animosity toward Maj. Gen. William S. Rosecrans. He omitted any reference to his infamous General Order 11 against the Jews. "That was a matter long past and best not referred to," he told Fred during edits.

He skirted other controversies, such as the late-war firing of Maj. Gen. Gouverneur K. Warren by one of his hand-picked proteges, Maj. Gen. Phillip Sheridan. Warren spent 20 years trying to clear his name but Grant, during his time as general in chief and then as president, passively resisted the effort in defense of Sheridan. Sheridan obstructed the effort even more, and by the time a court of inquiry cleared Warren of wrong-doing, Warren was dead.

**Grant could not lay down and so sat, slept, and wrote in a sitting position with his feet propped in a second chair positioned opposite the first.** (ac/cm)

The fierce loyalty Grant showed to his closest friends proved one of his greatest weaknesses. For instance, in part to defend Sherman's poor placement of troops and lack of vigilance at Shiloh, Grant forever denied the charge that Confederates surprised his army there, despite all evidence to the contrary. He instead diverted blame to Maj. Gen. Lew Wallace's late arrival to the battlefield on the first day of the battle. Wallace spent two decades trying to clear his name, and Grant only acknowledged the justness of Wallace's claims as a literal footnote in the *Memoirs.*

During the early days of the Overland Campaign, he backed Sheridan over Sheridan's boss, Meade, over the use of the army's cavalry, much to the army's detriment during the weeks that followed because Sheridan rode away with the army's eyes and ears.

Some of the scandals that later dogged Grant's presidency and tarnished his presidential legacy sprang from subordinates who took advantage of Grant's loyalty. Secretary of War William Belknap, for example, who had served under Grant in the war, was impeached for taking advantage of his office. Grant's

As Grant's publisher and friend, Mark Twain went to great lengths to protect Grant's interests. As two of America's most famous men, they shared a love of good stories and good cigars. (Note the cigar in Twain's left hand.) (loc)

private secretary, Orville Babcock, who had served on Grant's wartime staff, was indicted in an infamous scandal called "The Whisky Ring," which diverted tax revenue for illegal purposes. In both cases, Grant tried to defend his subordinates, letting friendship cloud his judgment on their actions.

Grant's legacy has been most tarnished, of course, by the rumors of excessive drinking that swirled around him at the time. The memoirs shed no light on that aspect of his life. Grant was a thoughtful man, but he was not introspective in his writing in that way, and so, although he shares many opinions about many people in his memoirs, he does not shine a bright light on his own interior life.

That has fallen to generations of historians, who have seen in Grant many things depending on the times. Lost Cause partisans savaged Grant's reputation early, and his reputation continues to suffer as a result. As he himself wrote in his memoirs, "Wars produce many stories of fiction, some of which are told until they are believed to be true." And so it happened with Grant: his enemies waged rhetorical war on him in such an unrelenting fashion that their fictions began to be accepted as truth.

Fortunately, beginning in the 1960s with historian Bruce Catton, Grant's military reputation began an upward reevaluation, although his presidential reputation lagged behind until a late-1990s surge in scholarship started a modern reappraisal that continues to this day.

For all that, Mark Twain declared *The Personal Memoirs of Ulysses S. Grant* "a literary masterpiece," and since its initial publication, it has never gone out of print. Grant's memoirs remain accessible, readable, and indispensable as a source for understanding the Civil War.

"[T]his war was a fearful lesson, and should teach us the necessity of avoiding wars in the future," Grant wrote. The cause, he concluded, "will have to be attributed to slavery." Three million people gained their freedom, and the Union itself gained *a new birth* of freedom. "It is probably well that we had the war when we did," Grant admitted. "We are better off now than we would have been without it, and have made more rapid progress than we otherwise should have made."

*    *    *

To celebrate the completion of his book, Grant and members of his entourage went for a short walk to a scenic overlook not far from the cottage where he was staying. Grant, too weak to walk himself, traveled in a special kind of wheelchair. As beautiful as the view was on that warm summer afternoon, the trip—only a few hundred yards—proved an ordeal. An exhausted Grant took to his bed as soon as they returned to the cottage, and he never got up.

On the morning of July 23, Grant's doctor stood at that same overlook, watching the sunrise, when a frantic voice called him to the cottage. Grant's condition had deteriorated steadily over the previous days, and death was near. The doctor called the family to assemble.

Grant lay in a bed in a downstairs room. Abraham Lincoln's portrait hung on the wall above the bed, while a presidential portrait of Grant hung elsewhere in the room. A soft breeze from the east stirred the curtains of the window opposite the bed, and "a white ray from the sun . . . reached across the room like a rod" and illuminated Lincoln's picture. According to the *New York Times*:

For more on Grant's final days and his effort to write his memoirs, read *Grant's Last Battle: The Story Behind the Personal Memoirs of Ulysses S. Grant* by Chris Mackowski, part of Savas Beatie's Emerging Civil War Series.

> *The light on the portrait of Lincoln was still sinking; presently the General opened his eyes and glanced about him, looking into the faces of all. The glance lingered as it met the tender gaze of his companion. A startled, wavering motion at the throat, a few quiet gasps, a sigh, and the appearance of falling into a gentle sleep followed. . . . He lay without motion. At that instant the window curtain swayed back in place, shutting out the sunbeam.*

It was 8:08 a.m. Thursday, July 23, 1885.

"Let us have peace."

# *Julia and Ulysses*

## APPENDIX A

### *BY LENA MOODY*

A quote from Julia, written in her memoir after Ulysses passed away, sums up perfectly their relationship:

> *For nearly thirty-seven years, I, his wife, rested and was warmed in the sunlight of his loyal love and great fame, and now, even though his beautiful life has gone out, it is as when some far-off planet disappears from the heavens; the light of his glorious fame still reaches out to me, falls upon me and warms me.*

Julia Boggs Dent was born January 26, 1826, to Colonel Frederick and Ellen Dent, at their home, White Haven, near St. Louis, Missouri. ("Colonel" was an honorary title, not a military one, common in the South.) She was the first girl after four boys. Three sisters came later, with one sister, Mary, dying in infancy.

From her earliest years, Julia was generous and warm hearted, qualities that were noted later in her life and cherished by Ulysses.

Julia attended the local school until she was ten years old. She was then sent to a private school in St. Louis, which was run by the Misses Mauro. She finished her studies in June of 1843, but chose to stay in St. Louis with Colonel Dent's cousin, Caroline (Mrs. John J. O'Fallon) until February of 1844.

When she returned to White Haven, Julia met Lieutenant Ulysses Grant for the first time. He had been visiting the Dent family about once a week since being stationed at Jefferson Barracks following his graduation from the United States Military Academy. Julia's brother, Frederick Dent, had been roommates with Grant at the Academy and invited him to visit

**While husband and wife were both independent individuals, the Grants felt most complete when together. (sl)**

**A statue of Julia Dent Grant stands outside the Grant Home State Historic Site in Galena, Illinois.** (loc/ch)

the family. After meeting Julia, Grant's visits became more frequent, and their courting began. One of Julia's traits that impressed Ulysses was Julia's horsemanship. She could ride as well as he, and they would take long rides and walks all through the countryside. He was also astonished at how easy it was for him to talk to her.

In May of 1844, Ulysses asked Julia to marry him, which she promptly declined, knowing that her father would object. She also felt she was too immature at that time. Colonel Dent could see no future in the marriage, believing Julia was too delicate for the rigors of the life of an army officer's wife. As fate would have it, with the Mexican War starting, they would have to wait four more years before marrying.

When Ulysses returned from the war in July of 1848, he again asked Colonel Dent for Julia's hand in marriage. This time, he consented to the union. Plans were put into place and, on August 22, 1848, the couple married in the Dent family town home in St. Louis. "I like that young man," Mrs. Dent said. "There is something noble in him. His air and the expression of his face convince me that he has a noble heart and that he will be a great man someday."

Ulysses's father, Jesse, and his mother, Hannah, refused to attend the wedding because they were abolitionists, and the Dents were slave owners. Also, they knew the couple would be visiting the Grants' home in Ohio on their honeymoon trip—a visit that lasted three months. The newlyweds then returned to White Haven.

Ulysses was soon ordered to join his regiment in Detroit, Michigan. Parting from her father and severing the bonds of home in late November, Julia felt overwhelmed. Ulysses was much disturbed and unhappy seeing her so upset. With his arm around her, he bent his head and whispered, "Dry your tears and do not weep again. It makes me so unhappy."

The couple joined the 4th Infantry in Detroit. Upon their arrival, Lieutenant Grant was promptly ordered to Madison Barracks in Sackett's Harbor, New York. When detailed for court-martial duty in nearby Oswego, he wrote to her from along the way. "I find that I love you just the same in Adams that I did in Sackets Harbor. A thousand kisses and much love to you," he wrote on Feb. 27. On March 1, in Oswego, he admitted, "I can not tell you anything except how *very very* much I love you and how often I think of you." She, in turn, would call him "the tenderest and sweetest of husbands."

Ulysses received orders to return to Detroit, but with the lake-effect winter in full swing along Lake Ontario, Ulysses asked permission to stay at Madison Barracks until the opening of easier navigation in the spring. "At this time no boats are running," he explained, "and I would therefore be obliged to make the trip most of the way bv stage with my family which at this season of the year is most insupportable for females." Permission was granted. The couple made many friends while in Sacketts Harbor, and they both enjoyed having company. During this winter of 1848–49, they settled into a deep pattern of happiness, which lasted all through their lives. Those were the days Julia came to know Ulysses and to give him her life-long devotion.

The Grants returned in early spring to Detroit and, by early summer, Julia traveled to White Haven to give birth to their firstborn child on May 30, 1850, a son she named Frederick Dent Grant, "Fred," after her father. During her absence, Ulysses was restless

Julia Grant suffered from an eye condition called strabismus, today referred to as "crossed eyes," as a result of "an accident in babyhood." As an adult, Julia often had her photograph taken in profile. In later 1863, as her husband's fame grew, she consulted a surgeon in St. Louis about having the condition corrected. When she told her husband, he replied, "What in the world would put such a thought in your head, Julia? . . . Did I not see you and fall in love with you with those same eyes? I like them just as they are, and now, remember, you are not to interfere with them. They are mine, and let me tell you, Mrs. Grant, you had better not make any experiments, as I might not like you half so well with any other eyes." "And I never did," Julia wrote in her memoirs, "my knight, my Lancelot!" (gc)

and lonely. He had found Julia to be a comforting and absorbing presence in his life, and he missed her greatly. This was the first of the periods in which he felt himself aimless and unhappy without her. After he had waited as long as he could stand it, Ulysses went to St. Louis to retrieve his wife and new son, and they returned to Detroit together. The small family stayed there until the following spring.

**Col. Frederick Dent (center) remained a central figure in Julia's life until his death in 1873. The colonel and his son in law did not often see eye to eye on issues, but Grant nonetheless sought his father-in-law's advice. Dent is pictured here with Julia, Nellie, and Jesse.** (loc)

In June of 1851, Ulysses and Julia gave much thought to their future. With his eight-year enlistment requirement about to end, they both knew that the life of a Quartermaster had little to offer him. Also, around this time, Ulysses learned that Julia was going to have a second baby.

In Sackett's Harbor, they had begun attending the Presbyterian church. Ulysses had also joined the Independent Order of Odd Fellows and the Sons of Temperance. He marched in torchlight parades and was elected to high office in the organization. Julia proudly hung his parchment membership certificate in their home. Julia saw in her husband—now 29 years old, restless, and obviously being used below his capacity—great things ahead for him.

It was her sunny disposition that helped him through hours of discouragement. She was clearly both an inspiration and a comfort to him. She had already developed a deep understanding of his capacities and basic needs. In the summer of 1852, Ulysses's regiment received orders to the Pacific Northwest. This would become another test and trial of their devotion and resilience.

After many tears, Julia conceded that, being pregnant, it was best she not go with him, but she clung to the hope that she would yet accompany him to California after she gave birth. Crossing the isthmus of Panama would be too dangerous for her and the children, one of whom would be a newborn. They decided that she should go to his parents' home in Bethel, Ohio, for the birth of the child. Ulysses bade farewell in the middle of June and left on the first leg of his trip. His regiment set sail from New York on July 5.

On July 22, 1852, their second child was born at the home of his parents. Julia named him Ulysses S. Grant, Jr., but he was immediately dubbed "Buck" because, it was said, "He is a son of the Buckeye State!" She and the children stayed in Bethel until the baby was six weeks old, when she traveled to St. Louis to stay at White Haven with her family while Ulysses was in the Pacific Northwest. She received letters from Ulysses in every returning mail.

While he was at Fort Vancouver, her first letter reached him telling him that he had a second son. She traced the outline of the infant's hands in pencil on the last sheet. It touched him to the quick.

Oftentimes, while reading letters from Julia, Ulysses's eyes filled with tears. On one such occasion, a sergeant's wife who kept house for the officers caught him crying. "Mrs. Sheffield," he said, "I have the dearest wife in the world, and I want to resign from the army and live with my family."

On April 11, 1854, Ulysses wrote two letters on the same day. One of them was a formal acceptance of his promotion to Captain, regular army. The other was a brief letter of resignation from the army. Finally, he was bound for home and family! Julia had faith in Ulysses and, knowing him better than anyone, she voiced her belief in him and said he was destined for big things.

On July 4, 1855, Julia bore her third child, and only daughter, Ellen "Nellie" Grant at Wish-ton-Wish, about three miles from White Haven. It was

During Grant's prewar service and during the Civil War, Julia lived at various times with her in-laws, Hannah and Jesse Grant. Times were not always harmonious. Writing in reply to a letter from Jesse, Grant complained, "all that comes from you speaks so condescendingly of everything Julia says, writes, or thinks. You . . . are so prejudiced against her that she could not please you. This is not pleasing to me." Julia even had troubles with Grant's sisters. "Such unmitigated meanness as is shown by the girls make me ashamed of them," Grant wrote his wife. (loc)

The Grants, with Julia seated at the center of family life. She and Ulysses relished their roles as parents, but they also relished their roles as husband and wife, completely devoted to one another. (loc)

the home of her brother, Louis, who had asked them to take over the property while he left for California. On February 6, 1858, the Grant's fourth and last child was born. It was another son, named Jesse Root Grant after Grant's father.

Through these troubled and hard times before the Civil War, the Grants' deep love for each other and the delight they took in their children was an illustration of their sturdy spirit. They were all at their best when they were together. Writing later to a prospective Grant biographer, Julia cautioned him not to believe gloomy stories about Grant's financial hardship in St. Louis before the Civil War. Those days "were not dark but bright and charming, as it was always sunshine when he was near." As was her nature, she put the happiest shine possible on even troubled times.

Once the Civil War began and Ulysses was back in the army, his true destiny, and the fame that Julia had known in her heart since their courting days, became a reality. When he became a brigadier general in August

LENA MOODY's *interest in the Civil War began when Curt decided to portray General U. S. Grant. While helping him research for the role, her interest in the individual people in the war and their personal stories became a passion. She later decided to portray Julia Grant to be beside the General and discovered, in her research, that she and Julia have very similar personalities. "We strive to inspire and encourage others to learn about the people of our past in order to be better people themselves," she says.*

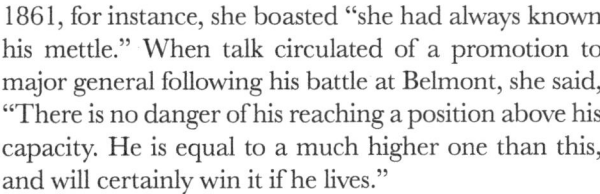

1861, for instance, she boasted "she had always known his mettle." When talk circulated of a promotion to major general following his battle at Belmont, she said, "There is no danger of his reaching a position above his capacity. He is equal to a much higher one than this, and will certainly win it if he lives."

In the summer of 1856 or 1857, Julia's mother had made a prophecy to Julia and Nellie, Julia's younger sister: "Remember what I say," Mrs. Dent told them. "That little man will fill the highest place in this government. His light is now hid under a bushel, but circumstances will occur, and at no distant day, when his worth and wisdom will be shown and appreciated. He is a philosopher. He is a statesman. You will all live to see it, but I will not." Mrs. Dent died January 14, 1857, and never got to see her son-in-law rise to general-in-chief of the army or president of the United States.

TOP LEFT: An 1872 photo captures Jesse striking a pose with his parents. (loc)

TOP RIGHT: As Grant's only daughter, Ellen "Nellie" Grant held a special spot in her father's heart. (loc)

BOTTOM RIGHT: An 1877 portrait of Ulysses S. "Buck" Grant, Jr. (loc)

# ULYSSES S. GRANT

## Primary Sources

*The Personal Memoirs of Ulysses S.
Grant: The Complete Annotated Edition*
Ulysses S. Grant
John F. Marszalek, et al., editors
(Belknap Press, 2017)
ISBN-13: 978-0674976290

*The Annotated Memoirs of
Ulysses S. Grant*
Ulysses S. Grant
Elizabeth D. Samet, editor
(Liveright, 2018)
ISBN-13: 978-1631492440

Grant's memoirs are widely available for free on the internet, and several handsome modern editions are available in print. Two annotated editions provide exceptional value-added to the memoirs by identifying people and places Grant mentions in his work and providing additional context to events. The tone and content of the annotations in each are dramatically different, making them excellent supplements to one another. Both editors come with excellent credentials: Marszalek and his team worked for the Ulysses S. Grant Presidential Library; Samet for West Point.

*Military History of Ulysses S. Grant* (3 vols.)
Adam Badeau
(D. Appleton & Co., 1868)
LCCN: 08034294

*Campaigning with Grant*
Horace Porter
(The Century Company, 1897)
LCCN: 02008573

*The Personal Memoirs of Julia Dent
Grant (Mrs. Ulysses S. Grant)*
Julia Grant (John Y. Simon, editor)
(Southern Illinois University Press, 1988)
ISBN-13: 978-0809314430

*Around the World with General Grant*
(2 vols.)
John Russell Young
(The American News Co., 1879)
LCCN: 05027038

## Secondary Sources

*The literature on Grant is huge–and growing every year thanks to an ongoing reevaluation of his military and political careers. A comprehensive list is impossible, but here is a selection of key works to explore.*

*Grant at 200: Reconsidering the Life and Legacy of Ulysses S. Grant*
Chris Mackowski and Frank Scaturro, editors
(Savas Beatie, 2023)
ISBN-13: 978-1611216141

*The Presidency of Ulysses S. Grant*
Charles W. Calhoun
(University Press of Kansas, 2017)
ISBN-13: 978-0700624843

*Grant*
Ron Chernow
(Penguin, 2017)
ISBN-13: 978-1594204876

*Let Us Have Peace: Ulysses S. Grant and the Politics of War and Reconstruction, 1861–1868*
Brooks D. Simpson
(University of North Carolina Press, 1997)
ISBN-13: 978-0807846292

*U. S. Grant: American Hero, American Myth*
Joan Waugh
(University of North Carolina Press, 2009)
ISBN-13: 978-0807833179

*American Ulysses: A Life of Ulysses S. Grant*
Ronald C. White
(Random House, 2016)
ISBN-13: 978-1400069026

## Additional Sources

*Curt has consulted literally dozens of primary and secondary sources to research his portrayal of Grant. Some of his favorites not detailed on the annotated bibliography:*

- *Grant of Appomattox* by William E. Brooks
- *The Trial of U. S. Grant* by Charles G. Ellington
- *The Generalship of Ulysses S. Grant* by J. F. C. Fuller
- *General Grant's Last Stand* by Horace Green
- *Ulysses S. Grant* by Robert R. McCormack
- *The War Without Grant* by Robert R. McCormack
- *The General's Wife* by Ishbel Ross
- *When General Grant Expelled the Jews* by Jonathan D. Sarna
- *Grant* by Jean Edward Smith

*For narrative storytelling, it's hard to beat "the Grant Trilogy": Captain Sam Grant by Lloyd Lewis; Grant Moves South by Bruce Catton; and Grant Takes Command by Bruce Catton*

# About the Authors

**Dr. Curt Fields** has had a strong interest in the Civil War since he was about 12 years old. That interest led him, ultimately, to portray General Grant in first-person. In "being" General and President Grant, he developed a deep respect for the complex man that Grant was—a man who has, regrettably, been shunted into the shadows of history. In the 21st century, Curt has been a police officer and hostage negotiator; a high school teacher and later a principal; and a university instructor. In 2022, he was elected to the board of

directors of the Ulysses S. Grant Association. He lives in Collierville, Tennessee, a suburb of Memphis.

**Chris Mackowski, Ph.D.,** is the editor-in-chief and co-founder of Emerging Civil War (www.emergingcivilwar.com). He is the series editor of the award-winning Emerging Civil War Series, and author, co-author, or editor of more than twenty-five books. Chris is a professor of journalism and mass communication in the Jandoli School of Communication at St. Bonaventure University in Allegany,

New York, and historian-in-residence at Stevenson Ridge, a historic property on the Spotsylvania battlefield in central Virginia.